PRAISE FOR *GO F*

"…showcases the spirit and mindset required to push yourself beyond your limits and achieve your dreams."
—**Dean Karnazes,** *New York Times* bestselling author of *Ultramarathon Man*

"This book will encourage you to live more adventurously. A practical, inspiring guide to help you make the most of life."
—**Pip Stewart,** author of *Life Lessons from the Amazon*

"…not only a how-to guide for a variety of engaging sports but also a step-by-step mastercourse on the mindsets therein."
—**Travis Macy,** author of *The Ultra Mindset*

"Jennifer Strong McConachie is a master of endurance and a skilled writer who shares her experiences with us so that we can take the principles of going far and apply them to our everyday life."
—**Jennifer Pharr Davis,** National Geographic Adventurer of the Year and author of *The Pursuit of Endurance*

"The reader will gain broad and heartfelt knowledge of their own place in the world of sport."
—**Scott Tinley,** author of *Finding Triathlon*

GO FAR

GO FAR

HOW ENDURANCE SPORTS HELP YOU WIN AT LIFE

Jennifer Strong McConachie

Hatherleigh Press is committed to preserving and protecting
the natural resources of the earth. Environmentally
responsible and sustainable practices are embraced
within the company's mission statement.

Visit us at www.hatherleighpress.com and register online
for free offers, discounts, special events, and more.

GO FAR

Text Copyright © 2021 Jennifer Strong McConachie

Library of Congress Cataloging-in-Publication Data is available.

ISBN: 978-1-57826-913-6

All rights reserved. No part of this book may be reproduced, stored
in a retrieval system, or transmitted, in any form or by any means,
electronic or otherwise, without written permission from the publisher.

Printed in the United States

10 9 8 7 6 5 4 3 2 1

CONTENTS

FOREWORD

In *Go Far*, Jennifer has taken what she has learned through trial and error, considered research, and her diverse experiences to formulate a complete life-training approach. These three elements—an Explorer's Mindset, Outlier Tactics and Immersion Theory—are practices which she embodies in everything that she does.

Jennifer has indeed 'gone far' in the multitude of sporting disciplines that she has embraced: from ultra-distance running, to open-water swimming, to mountaineering, hiking, adventure racing, multisport and self-constructed training adventures. But through it all, what strikes me most is not just her preparation or her willingness to participate in a diverse range of events, but the way that she wholeheartedly embraces the culture, cuisine, history and art of every destination that she visits.

If you are a newcomer to exploring the great outdoors through sport and event participation, *Go Far* will open your eyes to what is out there for *you* to discover (activities, events, places), offer sound guidance around preparation, and steer you toward getting the most out of experiences and opportunities—in both life and sport.

Seasoned athletes will appreciate a nudge from Jennifer's insights; single-discipline athletes may find themselves tempted to broaden their horizons; while those who have been training and participating in events for decades will be reminded of those things that they may have forgotten, neglected, or stopped doing—for whatever reason.

Expect to be inspired, energized, curious and ready to plan your next adventure after reading *Go Far*.

—Lisa de Speville, founder of Vagabond Kayaks
and author of *Adventure Racing*

INTRODUCTION

The Beginnings of Endurance

I am in the oldest desert in the world, preparing to climb up one of the highest sand dunes on record. It is mid-morning on the final day of a five-day desert stage race. The sand is deep orange, ancient. I run across the veld approaching the pile of massive dunes that must be summited before the race is complete. I have already covered 108 miles, running for six, seven, eight hours a day in 120-degree temperatures.

A few months ago, I didn't even know there was a country called Namibia. Today I am surrounded by its vastness. I am on the other side of the world somewhere in the back of beyond. I approach the sandy foothill and climb—fingers and feet swooshing deep into the ruddy sand. It is so steep that near the top, I crawl on all fours. I am one with the earth. I am connected with my body and my soul to nature in her most basic element. I tell myself this is what it means to be alive.

My name is Jennifer. I am a life-long endurance athlete in sports like running, wild swimming, mountaineering, paddling, triathlons, adventure racing and multisport. I am a wife, a mother, a Siberian husky parent, and now a writer. This book is a culmination of what I have experienced in more than 30 years of competing in endurance sports and living an adventurous life. I am an ordinary person with an extraordinary approach to fitness, life and training.

In this book, I cover my standout way to tackle big ideas and grand goals. I share what it takes to be a multidisciplinary endurance athlete who has traveled the globe, raced an ultra-marathon on five of the seven continents, swam the Hellespont from Europe to Asia, escaped Alcatraz, climbed several of the Seven Summits, and conquered an American epic by running across the Grand Canyon and then back again.

In these pages, I share how to find immersive global experiences from your front door to exotic locales around the world. I hope my journey inspires and teaches you how to connect with nature and seek adventure to become a confident winner physically, mentally, emotionally and spiritually.

I apply the principles I have learned competing and training in endurance sports to excel in business and life. Tackling endurance challenges can help you personally and professionally as you learn to take on adversity, combat stress and, most importantly, have fun. Endurance challenges like climbing the tallest mountain on a continent, running 100 miles, and swimming through the cold waters of the Baltic Sea taught me resiliency and persistence. I learned how to seek out new experiences and opportunities to succeed. I do this as a normal, non-professional athlete, without the backing of sponsors or excessive natural ability, but with a three-tiered life approach.

I am excited to share this pilgrimage with you, so you can use these principles of endurance in your life as well.

PART I

Creating a Life Approach

Run long
Climb high
Swim deep
Go far

By participating in extreme events around the globe, like climbing mountains, running volcanoes, trekking deserts, hiking canyons, bushwhacking jungles and swimming seas, I have experienced the enduring power of nature and the tenacity of the human spirit, while living out some of my life-long dreams. My endurance training approach helped me combine the abilities and resources I had within myself to make my goals into realities. Research continues to show that competitive and extreme sports improve focus and work output. Endurance sports can help you achieve more inside and out. The journey that you go on can be transformative. I want to help you cultivate what you have inside yourself and what resources are available to you in order to find adventure in your everyday life.

I have been a runner and endurance athlete my entire life. This is not a story about someone who one day in her 20s started running and turned out to be great at it. If that is you, I am envious! There was no overnight success for me, only years of trial, error, training, experimenting and, yes, blood, sweat and more often than not, tears. Through those years of training, I have worked to develop my talents and skills into something that I can share to help others.

If you are an amazing athlete, an average athlete, or someone who has not yet entered the world of sports, I want you to know that you can find ways to win at life through the mindset I use for endurance sports training in my life.

I want to teach you to mobilize the skills you uncover with this information to help you win in the way that feels successful to you. You don't have to be a top-of-the-field athlete or businessperson to triumph in outdoor exploits or your professional life. You only need three things. These three things helped me become the person I am. My wish is that they also help you. These three pillars are my standout life training approach I use to find the fun in my training and my daily life.

Three-Pillared Life Approach:

1. Develop an Explorer's Mindset
2. Use Outlier Tactics
3. Practice Immersion Theory

By developing an Explorer's Mindset, using Outlier Tactics and practicing Immersion Theory, you can create a life full of adventure and success.

In the following chapters, I will define each of these pillars and give you specific steps and examples on how to apply them. I will also share stories from my adventures and how developing these tools has allowed me to succeed in any condition—from the freezing cold to the boiling heat to the wilds of the backcountry.

1 | Pillar I: Develop an Explorer's Mindset

Developing an Explorer's Mindset is the first step of my life approach. Developing an Explorer's Mindset means you find ways to seek out discovery, adventure and freedom in your life. By taking on the mindset of a can-do, try-new-things explorer, I traveled the world competing in running, swimming, mountain, and adventure racing events, often training for several simultaneously. I learned about the lands around me and became a citizen of the world.

Developing an Explorer's Mindset involves taking five key steps:

1. Seeking out discovery, adventure and freedom
2. Curating the right attitude
3. Building multilateral personal development
4. Always be treasure hunting
5. Applying the Shopping Cart Test to your daily life

For me, my Explorer's Mindset training started right away. To explore means to travel over new territory for adventure or discovery. I was lucky to be raised in an environment that supported and encouraged self-discovery mixed in with a little adventure. My mom and dad helped nurture my love for reading, movement, getting outdoors and a sporting lifestyle from an early age.

I spent my childhood running road races and competing in triathlons around the Midwest. It started with my dad finding fun, active things for us to do together as a family. I was also a competitive club swimmer for 10 years because I loved being in the water and how empowered the underworld of liquid made me feel.

I grew up surrounded by this can-do, try-new-things, be-outside, personal-development-focused attitude. Hailing from America's heartland anchored me with a strong sense of place, mixed with an individualistic self-reliance that united me with the lands around me. I always felt connected to my home state of Kansas and its pioneering history. As a kid, my favorite books were Laura Ingalls Wilder's *Little House on the Prairie* series; I always wanted to learn more about the outside world around me and how people survived in past centuries.

I liked to study our giant geographical atlas full of maps of the world in our library room packed with encyclopedias, reference books, biographies and stories of the world's famous adventures, explorers and novelists. The antique maps lived next to our Kansas road atlas and Colorado backpacking guides. As a child I would pour over topographies, globes and compendiums to far-off places on our always-overflowing bookshelves.

If it had to do with nature, sports, fitness, health or adventure, we were in. We hiked and walked and spent our summers at the pool. We had a tightrope in our backyard and a trapeze. My dad built obstacle courses for me full of gymnastics equipment, a clubhouse, a fort and stilts. When I became interested in aerial arts, my parents surprised me with my own silver hooped lyra. There once was even a bed of nails. Bikes, boats, inventions and projects crowded our garage and racing numbers from past events lined the walls.

We got up early, found new things to try and new ways to do them. We explored our neighborhood, our city, our state, the Midwest, the United States and the world, following our interests. We tried every sports nutrition bar and healthy food trend, with my mom cooking new dishes to feed our active lifestyle and buying specialty ingredients from the health food store to keep up with the newest craze. Discovery was part of my everyday life—discovery of new places, foods, sports and strength inside myself from participating in those things.

I have heard it said that all families should have a river that they learn and explore. We had two—the Big Arkansas and the Little Arkansas rivers.

In the spring, my best friends and I would watch fireworks along the banks, walking over early in the day to set up blankets. In the evening, we would unpack our snacks and fall asleep in our parent's laps under the erupting sky. In the winter we neighborhood kids would bundle up and walk down to the annual star and Christmas tree lighting while singing Christmas carols. In the fall I learned how to canoe, sail, row and kayak in the waters. In the summer, when the waters would recede, we would hike down and gather mussels from the muck, wearing my mom's old rain boots. In between, we ran wild, collecting the flora and fauna of our neighborhood's hideaways as free-range kids, only showing up back at home for meals or sleepovers. Later, in high school cross county, after college and in my professional life, I would run the rivers, to their beginnings and ends, discovering their many secrets. Today I still run them.

I loved studying how people lived, exploring the past. Throughout Wichita, Kansas, history, people have always used the rivers of the Arkansas for recreation. I looked at old photos of Victorian women in white, canoeing, picnicking and stealing kisses under the trees of the same park I ran, biked and kayaked through. On the Little Arkansas River, I rowed past the old boathouse where people waterskied and jumped off a roof tower diving board. The Big Arkansas River had an amusement park on a sandbar island in the middle of it in the early 1900s. Before Wichita was a city, Native American communities would gather at the confluence of the Big Arkansas and Little Arkansas rivers to trade goods. The more I studied Wichita history, the more I felt a connection with my past and with the rivers. Waters and rivers have always embodied the spirit of discovery. While on the river I like to quote the famous water adventurers of Lewis and Clark, Huck Finn, Joseph Conrad, and the animals of *The Wind in the Willows*.

Books about rivers are always the best books.

Discovery, Adventure & Freedom

Seeking out discovery, adventure and freedom—not like a tourist, but like a true explorer—is the first step in developing an Explorer's Mindset.

When I was seven, I ran my first race on a winding park road nestled between my two Arkansas rivers, in an oversized white T-shirt and hot color running shorts en vogue in 1990. It was a two-mile fun run, and I remember it not being a lot of fun. In fact, I remember thinking, "Running is hard."

Not much has changed; running is still hard, but I have learned to love it because it is hard. I added in longer distances and disciplines along the way with encouragement from my parents. Getting into long and hard endurance sports as a young person was a natural evolution of finding exciting, ahead-of-the curve family activities.

This focus on discovery and adventure brought my child-hood to life. It can help you by allowing you to discover new sports, activities, foods and life approaches, and by helping you find freedom and adventure via an Explorer's Mindset.

With the right attitude, you can wake up and have new adventures every day. By approaching each day with an Explorer's Mindset, you can learn, discover and grow through new experiences.

An Explorer's Mindset means you are open to new possibilities and that you look for new possibilities. You look for ways to add exploring to your daily life.

For example, go somewhere you have never been before. This doesn't have to be an epic across-the-seas adventure. You can start in your own neighborhood. Now. Today. You can walk right out of your front door and go out and see new things. You can travel over new territory where you are now. This is what adventure is all about.

I have approached my endurance and life training with the question: Why run when you can have an adventure run? That is what makes running fun and why I keep doing it. You can also try a new sport, like packrafting. Try two or three together, like an aquathon, duathlon, biathlon or triathlon. There are always new books to read and sagas to tackle. Go to a new restaurant or venue. Try a new food. Try a new fruit or vegetable. I have a goal of trying new produce in all the countries I travel to. Go to a new part of town or drive through a small town that you have never been to on the way to somewhere else. Walk, run or bike to that small town. Find a destination and make a plan on how to get there by your own propulsion. Go to a deeper place physically, mentally, emotionally and spiritually by training, traveling, reading and testing yourself. Endurance sports will help take you there. Near or far, there are always things to discover.

Applying this method of discovery to my years of running has kept it fresh and interesting. No one wants to run 5ks forever; having run 5ks my whole childhood, I didn't want to run them again in my 20s. I wanted something new and different. That was ultrarunning, travel and the famous summits of the world. Each of these experiences allowed me to explore new countries and create new, enriching life discoveries.

The secret to finding freedom and adventure in life is to explore.

Think about being alive on an open road running. Or swimming in a greenish blue lake. Imagine the famous explorers of old sailing on the high seas to new lands.

This is freedom from the cage of society and its expectations. Adventure sports can bring you freedom to find your inner thoughts and your own path through life's challenges.

I go out and explore my world because it makes me feel alive. It teaches me new things about life and life happening around me. I want to experience the world fully, and how better to do so than being out in all of nature's true elements.

One of the key elements of exploring is discovery. Discovery includes uncovering something new, but it can also include uncovering something old. In order to be open to discovery, you have to have the right attitude.

Curating the right attitude is step two in developing an Explorer's Mindset. As a child I was raised with a can-do attitude. My parents empowered me to find new things to do, try them, and take them on. This way of looking at the world encouraged me to seek out what I was interested in and pursue it. As I grew up, I took this can-do, try-new-things attitude on as my own. I liked that it allowed me to explore and discover the world by testing it out, trying it and jumping in. It helped me problem solve and look for new opportunities. A can-do attitude made me feel confident. It helped me stay committed to my goals throughout my life, because I looked at the things I wanted to achieve in a positive manner.

I competed in running races almost every weekend growing up. When my dad found a rollerblade race in a nearby town, we signed up along with a coterie of my neighborhood, swimming and triathlon friends. A rollerblade race was outside of my comfort zone, but I was excited and energized to try it. Similarly, as an adult, when I had the chance to travel to the country of Namibia to run for five days straight across a desert, I approached the challenge with a can-do mental attitude because I wanted to travel to a new part of the world and I wanted to learn what I was capable of. Could I learn a whole new way of running, competing and surviving? The only way to find out was to try. Curating a can-do attitude allowed me to take on new things, from new sports to new work challenges to global adventures.

Curiosity is a key factor in having a can-do attitude. By staying curious, you can follow that curiosity to pursue what you are interested in. You can follow your interests to build out your sense of self via personal development.

Building in multilateral personal development is step three in developing an Explorer's Mindset. Personal development goes hand-in-hand with having a can-do attitude. When you have the right attitude, looking for new things to try comes naturally. Trying new things helps you grow as a person and develop more fully.

Personal development allows you to build your identity. It brings awareness to who you are as a person and where you can improve.

The great thing about personal development is that it can be in any area. Physically, it might be new sports, races or sporting racing combinations, like the Scandinavian SwimRun I tried when it was on the cusp of becoming a new, popular sport. You can also seek out ways to push yourself to grow mentally by learning new skills, abilities, talents and hobbies; spiritually by finding deeper ways to walk in your faith; and emotionally by testing yourself as you take on adversity and the challenges of life and relationships.

By building multilateral personal development into each of these four areas, physical, mental, emotional and spiritual, I was always pushing myself by learning. I sought out themes that interested me enough to delve into. I focused not just on my sporting lifestyle, but on growing as a person, at work in business, and spiritually and emotionally.

Endurance sports served as an intersection for these four areas and a base from which to build more ways to grow.

Multilateral personal development encourages well-rounded individuals. When you are balanced and pushing toward the best in each of these areas, physical, mental, emotional and spiritual, your quality of life will improve, because you are always learning, trying and doing a variety of activities in a variety of areas.

For example, as I became a global athlete, I also wanted to become a global citizen. I wanted my journey to be not only about the physical, but about the mental, emotional and spiritual sides of my life as well, so I used ultrarunning, swimming mountaineering and adventure racing as ways to travel, explore the world and learn about new cultures.

I prepared for each trip by reading books and watching movies about the area I was embarking to. I listened to music and songs about the region. I studied the geography, maps, and planned sights to see, how to best see them, what fun activities to do, and what and where to eat. I made a list of 20 different specialty foods unique to New Zealand to try when I traveled there for a forest ultrarun, like lamington and hokey pokey vanilla ice cream strewn with pieces of honeycomb. I cooked foods from the countries I traveled to like a *Pastel de Choclo* Chilean casserole after a trip to Patagonia. By preparing and researching, I created immersive global experiences before, during and after a trip to learn about new places as well as traveling to them. I wanted to be an informed global citizen. I read the current news and cultural history of new and different countries. I would train, study, try, do, see, watch and taste defining parts of a new culture, while tapping into themes across media. I read novels about places and decided, "That would be a great place to go for an ultrarun!"

Now that we have learned the importance of seeking out discovery, adventure and freedom, curating a can-do attitude, and building in multilateral personal development, we can apply the fourth step in developing an Explorer's Mindset.

Treasure Hunting

When I kayak, bike or run, I find ways to include lakes and rivers, portaging, rapids, and treasure hunting. There is something that everyone wants to discover. That is Treasure.

Always be treasure hunting is the fourth step in developing an Explorer's Mindset.

What is treasure hunting? Treasure hunting is finding something new or old, unique or special to you. It is information, fact or possession you didn't used to have. Some of the treasures I have found over the years include sea glass in the Gulf of Finland, rocks full of mica on a Colorado hiking trail, a suitcase in the middle of the Big Arkansas River, a keyboard on the bike path, shells, glass bottles, pottery and, perhaps best of all, money in a hole that was fished out by my dad and me with a chewed up leftover gum collection, attached to a dowel rod and picked up from the hole by adhesion. Treasure is something hidden that is uncovered. By you. It doesn't matter what it is. What matters is that you found it.

My Siberian husky embodies the spirit of treasure hunting. That is why he craves his daily walks and runs. He wants to go out and find new things. In his case, this is often strange, discarded food or abandoned clothing. But when he seizes his newest prize, he gets a kick in his step and races home to enjoy his new possession, such as a frozen strawberry éclair bar. He is excited about discovery. I like to take this vein of enthusiasm and integrate it into my own life approach.

You can treasure hunt anywhere and you should always be on the lookout for treasure hunting possibilities. Fritz the husky does just this. He embraces the hunt for opportunity, finding new-to-him discoveries on every outing. Being always on the lookout for treasure can inspire us in our own lives and encourage us to get out.

When I went sailing in the British Virgin Islands, a chain of volcanic islands in the Caribbean, I swam to Treasure Island and collected fossil shells from its banks for my shell collection. I was on Treasure Island treasure hunting! What was even better was that I was reading the adventure book *Treasure Island* while I was there. I knew I would be traveling to the island on my trip, so I planned to read the children's classic full of pirates and seafaring drama, while sailing on those seas myself. I was able to bring my world of treasure to life with a story, a sail, a swim and a hunt.

The finest thing about treasure hunting is that you get to discover something. This might be a shell on an island jutting steeply out of the Caribbean aqua waters covered in dense dark green vegetation or an old glass bottle dug out from your local riverbank. It might be a story in a book that relates to a news article or a word you saw in a show that then popped up in a movie you watched. Discovery knits our world together. Here is an example:

When I was preparing for my Escape From Alcatraz swim through San Francisco Bay, I started researching other classic prison escape swims like the Freedom Swim off Robben Island in South Africa, or one from a favorite story of mine, The Chateau D'If from *The Count of Monte Cristo*.

I found another swim in French Guiana with fascinating colonial, maritime and prisoner history. Then I found a nonfiction, true-story book about escaping from that very prison in French Guiana. In that same turn, I learned about an old movie. The next day, while I was at the theater, I saw a preview for a remake of that old movie. The signs were mounting.

I started thinking about doing the Escape From Devil's Island Swim in French Guiana and knew I had to watch the 2017 movie *Papillon* I had just seen the preview for, and the 1973 original, and read the book, and then the sequel as well, to bring these discovery connections to life. They coincided in my life all at once to help me learn something arresting and new.

This is what I love about having an Explorer's Mindset: It shows you how discovery connects the threads of life. Whether it is finding a way to connect a river to a lake to a portage on an adventure race, or when history, interests, books, movies and prison escapes via swims all come together.

Do you want to find out if you have a treasure hunting spirit? Use the Shopping Cart Test.

The Shopping Cart Test

The Shopping Cart Test will help you determine how open you are to discovering treasure in your daily life. If you learn that you are not as open as you could be, you might find that the Shopping Cart Test can inspire your training, your routine, and even in business when seeking out new opportunities. The fifth step in developing an Explorer's Mindset is applying the Shopping Cart Test to your daily life.

One day, my dad came home with an old-school-style, oversized, upright shopping cart. He found it on a jobsite and brought it home for the neighborhood kids to play with. After that, we spent all of our free time loading it with treasures, then defined as our stuffed animals, and pushing our cart up and down our block, even taking it to a nearby museum and letting it fly down the steep, all-glass entrance when we were feeling up for a thrill.

This first shopping cart set up a lifetime of knowing how rousing and fortuitous shopping carts can be for the young at heart. I learned the lure of a shopping cart early. Did you?

Let's see. If you see a dumpster filled with interesting things, do you:

1. Keep driving, or running, not noticing the overflowing dumpster in the neighborhood.

2. Think to yourself, "Hmm, what is going on there?" Then go inside and forget.

3. Wait until it gets dark. Go down to the dumpster. Hang around long enough to see if the interesting things you want happen to fall out. Push those two very cute, very interesting, very fun shopping carts—one is never enough—down the street back to your garage.

If you answered number 3, then congratulations—you pass the Shopping Cart Test. You have a treasure hunting spirit. If you answered number 1 or 2, then you now know you can work to develop more treasure hunting in your life.

Applying the Shopping Cart Test to your daily life brings out your Explorer's Mindset. If it is through hunting treasure, swimming to and from islands, uncovering new information, or running outside, exploring the world, looking for treasure, this test can help you find what makes you happy. It can help you learn about yourself and understand your motivations, strengths and weaknesses. It can also make you free to be yourself and an individual. This test can help you learn how adopt the right attitude and define your personal interests you want to pursue to continue growing as a well-rounded person.

Seeking out discovery, adventure and freedom, curating a can-do attitude, building in multilateral personal development physically, mentally, spiritually and emotionally, always treasure hunting and applying the Shopping Cart Test to your daily life are the steps you can take to develop an Explorer's mindset. This is the first pillar to creating an endurance sports life approach that helps you win.

2   Pillar II: Use Outlier Tactics

Using Outlier Tactics is step two of my limit-pushing life approach. Outlier Tactics draw on big ideas outside the normal realm of thinking that encourage you to act differently.

Being an outlier means you are independent. You use this independent spirit to come up with new ideas outside the traditional range. You don't mind being outside the pack and thinking differently than the herd. You push boundaries and don't accept the status quo. Being an outlier means being ahead-of-the-curve and outside the norm.

Tactics here are a set of tools and strategies I use to implement my outlier thinking. Outlier Tactics allow you to plan to achieve big dreams by thinking, training and acting differently than the average athlete or businessperson.

I used my Outlier Tactics as tools to train and prepare for intense global adventures like dessert crossings and climbing mountains covered in ice, all from America's Heartland. I also used Outlier Tactics to get jobs and win clients. Outlier Tactics are all about employing new strategies to solve problems.

The Outlier Tactics in my adventure endurance arsenal include:

1. Coming up with ideas outside the norm

2. Adopting the 24-hour clock

3. Beating the day and winning the night

4. Seizing opportunities for adversity training

5. Creating new ways to administer the What
    Makes You Test

On a blustering winter day my freshman year in high school, my dad and I walked down to watch a collegiate regatta on the Little Arkansas River. It was on that day that I decided I wasn't going to run or swim in college. I had been a competitive runner and swimmer since I was seven years old. Why would I not stick with sports that I knew and was comfortable with? Instead, I was ready to try something else. I was going to master a new sport and row on the Kansas State University crew team. Running and swimming might have been inside the norm for me, but I wanted something different.

Division I collegiate athletics were demanding and all-consuming. I learned how to row on my Little Arkansas River as a young person and began to master the technical sport and new world of skull boats at K-State. After a year as a collegiate athlete, I again decided to pivot my sports life path. I wanted to have the time to get certified and to teach group fitness classes in my college town. I also found that the days where we ran and swam at rowing practice were my favorites. After an indoor team triathlon, I decided to return to competing in a sport from my youth that used my endurance training most efficiently. By returning to triathlons, I could use my swimming and running skills, my new power from rowing, and go back to a sport I was naturally good at, instead of continuing to struggle my way through rowing that I ended up not enjoying all that much. I was ready to dive back into the world of triathlon racing. In between, I became a certified group fitness and yoga instructor and added in adventure and multidiscipline races. I was back to multisport.

I was happy because instead of being solely focused on one sport and one thing, like collegiate rowing, I now got to focus on personal development from physical, mental, emotional and spiritual angles, as I trained in multiple sports, disciplines and varieties of fitness that fulfilled all my developmental goals.

I spent those college summers competing in triathlon distances like sprints, long course, Olympic and half-Ironmans. I increased my swimming, biking and running in between training for off-road and adventure races. One weekend, I raced an off-road Xterra triathlon one day, which consisted of lake swimming, mountain biking, and trail running. Then the following day, I came up with the outlier idea to race the sprint triathlon too, the very next day. It consisted of lake swimming, road biking and road running. This combination of an-off road triathlon on Saturday and a road triathlon on Sunday, when no one else at the event or anyone I knew had ever considered doing two different kinds of triathlons, two days in a row, because of the different discipline training, physical effort and gear required, was an example of early outlier thinking, which informed my Outlier Tactics approach that I was amassing one renegade idea at a time.

These were the beginning days of adventure racing in the early 2000s. I competed in trail running, always-muddy mountain biking, kayaking, canoeing, trekking, orienteering, lake and river swim crossings, rappelling, navigation and obstacle challenges, all linked together in a race, throughout the Midwest and South in between many on- and off-road triathlons.

My adventure racing distances included sprints at two to three hours, middle distances at 5–12 hours, and my favorite, the 24-hour. I was usually scratched, bruised and scarred from bushwhacking, rock scrambling and mountain bike falls because these races were always somewhere far away from civilization in the untamed lands of hazard, overgrowth and wildlife. My favorite thing about adventure racing was being in the trees and anytime I had the opportunity to get wet from a storm or water crossing. I also liked the added element of chance from the navigation portions. In a triathlon, the course was most always measured and marked. In adventure racing, part of the adventure was you never really knew where you were going and if you were getting there correctly. It heightened the stakes of the race.

Little did I know then that I was building up my arsenal of Outlier Tactics that I would later use in my life and for ultrarun training that would take me around the world.

After running my first marathon, at the age of 26 (for 26.2 miles, I had always had a goal of running a marathon at this matching age), I jumped into the world of ultrarunning with guidance from my father. He had the outlandish idea that if we were already trained for running 26.2 miles, we should stay trained instead of immediately stopping running after our race, and do a 50km/31-mile ultra one month later.

Coming up with ideas outside the norm is step one of using Outlier Tactics.

I implemented this step one of being an outlier when I decided to jump into ultrarunning right after my first marathon. At this time running ultras was still a relatively new idea and my dad was the only person I knew who had done one.

Coming up with a big, way-out-there idea that you talk about out loud, make a plan to achieve, and then work at every day to make your goal a reality, is how you use Outlier Tactics to come up with ideas outside the norm and turn those ideas into actions.

Saying your goals out loud can help you achieve these types of big dreams. It is one thing to have the idea. It is another thing entirely to do it. Saying your goals out loud can be a way of communicating your goal and helping you talk through your way of working through something big.

We all have ideas that seem too grand or too crazy. Thinking differently, like an outlier, can help you come up with ways to make these ideas doable. Think, "How can I do this," rather than, "I can't do this." I was raised always with this how-can approach and it has helped me work through my big, crazy, outlandish ideas and make them into realities. Rather than my parents saying, "No, you can't do that," or "We can't do that," we always worked as a team to problem-solve, get creative and figure out how we could make our ideas happen.

Talking about your goals and saying them out loud can help you articulate what you want to achieve and why you want to achieve it. When you understand your motivations, you learn how to motivate yourself through training and long events of the racing kind or the daily long-day-at-work or home kind.

Saying your goal out loud can also help formulate your plan on how to reach it. By talking through your goal and the process, you can see what you need to do and how you might go about doing it. You can evaluate what your strengths and weaknesses might be and how to use and overcome those.

If your goals are big enough, it is okay to fail along the way. I am an average athlete who has placed first in events and last in others. It feels great to be the best at something. It doesn't always feel great to be last at something, but the times when I have placed last in an event, I have always been happy to finish despite the extreme conditions I was under. When other competitors quit running a 100-mile race, had to be pulled out of the water during an ocean crossing, chose to go back down a mountain during a blizzard, or had to seek medical help during an island-crossing run covered in hazy sands blowing in from the Sahara Desert, I was always thankful to be able to find a way to keep going. It was okay that I wasn't the best at something because I was doing something so extreme, so out there, so big, that a lot of people had to quit during it—had to be rescued by boat—got injured and had to spend the remainder of the race in the medical tent—or even in extreme circumstances, had to be medically evacuated via private helicopter out of the Grand Canyon.

The price of grand goals is not always making your goal.

You have to decide that you don't care what other people think. To have true success, you have to decide that you are self-motivated and you are motivated by self-achievement. Set your goal, work toward, it, and if you fail, at least you tried and gave it everything you had. It is even all right to come in last place! This is all part of having big goals.

Using Outlier Tactics teaches you that it is not always about being the best athlete. It is not always about being first or fast. This approach teaches you that it is about going out, showing up, and using what you have to do what you can.

After my 50k run, I started doing more and more ultras, building up distances and eventually running ultras around the world and competing in multi-day stage racing for several years, while also learning mountaineering skills, climbing three of the Seven Summits, and competing in open-water swimming endurance events.

Along the way, I learned that being an endurance athlete was teaching me discipline that I could apply to all the other areas of my life. It taught me how to keep going no matter what.

The secret was to find the fun.

I used Outlier Tactics to do that.

The 24-Hour Clock

The second Outlier Tactic in my stockpile is adopting the 24-hour clock.

Growing up I had to get up early for swim practice. I was good at it, but I wanted to be better. I wanted to be one of those people who was ready to go any time day or night. I wanted to be good at not getting sleep. I wanted to live on the 24-hour clock. By expanding my idea of a day from 12 hours to 24 hours, I could train in the time I had, compete in crazy events, and do hard things, whether I got sleep in those 24 hours or not.

Collegiate rowing taught me how to get up even earlier and work on the water in all elements, including a squall that we rowed through, falling out of, and almost sinking, an eight-person skull on a freezing day in November, and racing on the water with wet socks, too big shoes, missed meals, mean coaches, little sleep and the heat, wind and cold prevalent on Kansas, Iowa and Texas lakes. I pushed myself to my limits even more so than high school sports, as everyday was a competition with not just myself but with my fellow teammates and the other college teams in the Big 12.

Swim practice and college rowing set me up early as a morning person. Later in life, adventure racing, ultrarunning, and mountaineering taught me how to be on a 24-hour schedule by officially adopting the 24-hour clock.

By adopting the 24-hour clock, I had 24 hours in a day to use. I expanded my thinking about working out or racing only in the morning or evening by expanding my definition of what morning and evening were. By adding in hours of the day that were usually reserved for relaxing, recovering, cooking, eating, socializing, or sleeping, I learned how to run all night to beat the heat of 100-degree Kansas summers. I went to bed at 9 pm, woke up at 1 am, and then ran through the night for nine hours into the next day. Similarly, I could get up and go at 2 am, 3 am or 4 am to run, paddle, bike and train.

When adopting the 24-hour clock, combat naps are a key skill you can use to persevere through sleeplessness. After I adopted the 24-hour clock, I could combat nap any place, any time.

A combat nap is a physical and mental break that you take in the midst of your current taxing activity. Combat naps can be anywhere from one minute to 20. They can be as short or as long as the time you have. You can lie all the way down, lean up against something, or sit still with your eyes closed. The key to combat napping is snatching the rest you can get in the moment to prepare you to continue on during the next moment. Combat naps helped me cross the Grand Canyon rim to rim to rim and they are also incredibly helpful in the world outside of running. They can be the secret to getting through long days of all kinds. Sometimes all you need is a mini mental and physical break to reignite your drive and dedication to your task at hand. Close your eyes. Rest your body. Recap what you have been through if you want, and visualize for the activity to come, or simply find rest when you can. Then get up and keep going.

Another component of the 24-hour clock is the alpine start. I learned the alpine start of mountaineering, going to bed at 6 pm and waking up at midnight, to climb into the dark, cold night up the summits of massive snow-and-rock covered mountains on Mount Kilimanjaro, Mount Rainer and Mount Elbrus in Russia.

I further pushed the sleeplessness training on my first 24-hour adventure race where I trekked, kayaked and biked for 24-hours, even with a concussion. During my first 100-mile run, I ran for 29 hours straight with no breaks to close my eyes or rest for even a second. The 24-hour clock allowed me to push past the bounds of one day and focus instead on the adventure at hand.

I used the 24-hour clock to get my hours of training in no matter if I was sick, tired, not feeling well or busy.

How did I go on matter how I was feeling? I was able to train through tired, busy and mild sickness because I put my hours in. Repetition became a pattern became a routine. Consistency, hard work and practice helped me get good at getting up and showing up. I put the time in and was dedicated even when it meant saying no to other things in my life.

The skill and commitment of living on a 24-hour clock opened up hours more of training possibilities. It didn't hurt either that I had a 24-hour dog. My Siberian husky was always ready to run day or night, rain or shine. It helped to wake up to a dog so excited he couldn't stop wooo-ing about it, bounding around the house, jumping, chasing his tail, and talking about running. Huskies like to talk and are known to be vocal. Mine was most expressive when getting ready to run. Leaving the house in the dark to run with Fritz would always wake me up and motivate me to go. He loved running so much it made me want to do it more for him than myself. His enthusiasm was catching.

Today, I can run, kayak, or hike any time of day or night, in any weather. I am on a 24-hour schedule from adopting the 24-hour clock. It is liberating and empowering. It was especially helpful after the birth of my daughter when I was up all night feeding and caring for her. I was experienced at being on for all hours of the day and night and surviving on combat naps—the perfect training for life and parenthood.

Beat the Day & Win the Night

Once you master the Outlier Tactic of being on a 24-hour clock, you can get up early. By getting up early, you can live an entirely additional life while most people are at home in bed sleeping. You can work toward goals, accomplish tasks, set a tone and focus for your day, and have exciting experiences you would otherwise miss. When you get up early, you beat the day and win the night.

Beating the day and winning the night is step three of using Outlier Tactics.

Beat the day by starting early, sometimes very early: Start a run at 9 pm or midnight if your long weekend training is taken up with other activities or plans. When you beat the day—the weather like hot temperatures or an incoming ice storm; a busy schedule; work or other impediments—you can use your 24-hour clock to go any time.

So, how do you win the night?

You win the night by getting comfortable in it; by getting accustomed to the dark.

I love being out at night. Time moves differently; both faster and slower. It might not be quiet. In fact, it is often noisy with the sound of bugs, cicadas and critters. But being out at night gives you a new perspective on life. It brings a stillness and a calm. Exploring my world from another angle, the nighttime, is fun and another way to be a part of life going on all around me. I like checking out a path I might run all the time or a road I might drive every day in the daylight in the dark. At night, everything is new. Night training is a different way to find adventure, explore, discover and be free.

Of course, you need to take proper safety precautions to do this, such as running with a training partner, using well-trafficked, lit, safe paths, and carrying protective gear and tools. But like with most things, it is worth it. If you want a change, try training for your usual sport, like swimming, biking, running or kayaking in the dark. You can find an entirely new, special world.

One cold, freezing night in January, it kept getting later and later, darker and darker and colder and colder. And I still needed to walk my husky to get his daily exercise needs in. I reluctantly bundled up and headed out into the night. The uninviting darkness surprised us with a light magical snowfall that fulfilled his inner canine spirit and mine and shocked us with its beauty. As we walked our empty neighborhood we got to connect with the outside world and we were rewarded with a scene out of a movie. As the snowflakes fell on his fur and my furry hood, everything gleamed under the white streetlight. We were happy. We were outside. We were cold (or I was at least) but we got to connect with the night by going out in it.

In the summer, I have gone out at midnight for bike rides to connect with the night. I have run all night for birthday night runs and all over town from one side to the other under the moon. Going out at night, in the dark added an element of newness to otherwise routine life and training.

Adversity Training

Seizing opportunities for adversity training is the fourth step in using Outlier Tactics. With the 24-hour clock, beating the day and winning the night, I knew I would eventually get enough sleep.

This fourth Outlier Tactic, adversity training, taught me I would also eventually get enough to eat and enough to drink. It might not be right when I needed it, but I would get it. Endurance events allowed me to learn this tactic. It is amazing how often it applies to other areas of my life, even a regular workday, or those early days of childrearing when it seemed like there was never enough time. Eventually, the seas would part, and I could come up from drowning in feedings, laundry, cleaning, tasks and to-dos. Knowing this is a key pillar in adversity training.

Running on the Kansas prairies has not always been easy. The hot and cold extremes have, however, helped me train for intense climates throughout the world.

If I look back at that stormy fall day at my first crew regatta, or trekking without water, with a contusion during a 15-hour adventure race, or racing an Ironman 70.3 in a rainstorm full of lightning, flooding shoes, and huddling under a hay barn for warmth in a spandex tri-suit, I can see the base being laid for my adversity training.

Adversity training is anything that makes your training harder like rain, ice, snow, wind, freezing mix, the cold, the heat, the humidity; waking up in the middle of the night to train; training under sleep deprivation; or on tired muscles; or through the tough parts of life like injury recovery, divorce, work projects, family stress, pregnancy and postpartum; adversity training is anything you have to problem solve around. It is running in inclement circumstances when you have no other choice but to endure them.

Rain is a great way to get your feet wet for adversity training. There is something magical about a rain walk. Even as a child I got inspired to gear up with a yellow jacket and blue rain boots to walk in the rain.

Rain runs are even better. So are rain swims, rain kayaks or rain hikes. I hiked the Inca Trail to Machu Picchu in Peru through four days of enveloping rain and green. I am always happy to be out in a storm. The most important thing to remember when in the rain is that once you get so wet, you can't get any wetter. As long as you know this, you can embrace a storm's cascading consummation. Rain and weather take your mind off the suffering and keep you alive and in the moment.

Weather makes a memory. One of my favorite runs ever was my junior year of high school at my final cross country race of the season. It was pouring down rain and our trails were covered in mud. I plowed through those puddles, splashing muck all over myself and the other runners, as fast as possible. There was no time to be careful or delicate. We were wet, muddy, and free to be wild in the rain.

Adversity training helps you get comfortable with being uncomfortable.

If you have ever ran at all, you are familiar with adversity training. You are familiar with being uncomfortable. It does not matter if you run one mile or 200, running is always hard. Running is the true adversity trainer.

The What Makes You Test

I have always been a runner. But what makes someone a runner? To answer that, I have a test that I have developed over the years.

What Makes a Runner:

1. You love running more than any other physical activity.

2. You compare everything else to running (hiking, climbing, mountaineering, biking, swimming, ballet, yoga, kayaking, rowing, etc.) As in, "This is so much easier than running,"

or "Running is so simplistic compared to this," or "This is this like running in fill-in-the-blank way."

3. You see someone running (even after a 4 AM pre-work 10-miler while you are comfortably cloistered in your car with your Starbucks) and think, "Oh, a runner! I wish I were running right now!"

So, are you a runner?

Either way, running has been my grounds for adversity training. The first element in adversity training is that you learn to run through it. Running through it is what makes you a runner.

Having a strong base as a runner has helped me try out and excel in other sports. The cornerstone of cardiovascular fitness and mental toughness that running requires has helped me swim faster and climb higher.

When you are adversity training you will find new, additional ways to incorporate the What Makes You Test. Coming back to this question, through the twists and turns of life, the true adversity trainer, will help you see how far you have come. When you create new ways to administer the What Makes You Test, the fifth step in using Outlier Tactics, be they wet, sleet, hail, squalls or storms, you know that you have properly embraced adversity training. You have accepted it and it will make you stronger.

Creating new ways to administer the What Makes You Test means you ask yourself frequently what you are made of. You make a habit of pushing yourself past boundaries. You decide to take on risks and find ways to overcome them. Preparing for

21-day overseas expeditions, like when I traveled to a conflict area to climb an ice-covered member of the Seven Summits, is risky. I had to prepare not just physically, but make sure that I was mentally strong, emotionally balanced, and spiritually fit to take on an otherworldly feat as well. By testing yourself by putting yourself in new situations, you can frequently evaluate and check in on what you are made of. That is the question the What Makes You Test asks, whether you are a runner or not.

Coming up with ideas outside the norm, adopting the 24-hour clock, beating the day and winning the night, seizing opportunities for adversity training, like embracing the rain, wet and all manner of weather events, and creating new ways to administer the What Makes You Test, by pushing yourself past boundaries, are the five ways you can use Outlier Tactics to accomplish hard things that require thinking differently to achieve and win at life.

3   Pillar III: Practice Immersion Theory

Immersion Theory is the third pillar in my life approach. Immersion means you absorb, become involved, and are extensively exposed to surroundings or conditions that are natively occurring around you. Theory means a set of ideal principles offered to explain phenomena, belief, policy or procedure. Practicing Immersion Theory means you engage fully and deeply in the environment around you by following a set of ideal principles. I am going to show you what these ideal principles are, so that you too can apply Immersion Theory to your life. These principles underline my phenomena, belief, policy and procedure that living an adventurous, endurance sports life will help you win mentally, physically, emotionally and spiritually.

Practicing Immersion Theory allowed me to accept whatever situation I was in, embrace it, and use it to my advantage. I used Immersion Theory to compete in some of the hottest, coldest and wettest places in the world, from aquamarine waters to dry yellows vleis to lush green rainforests to the planet's pinnacle perlite peaks. I also used it to create adventures from home by delving into the settings available to me.

The principles you can apply to practice Immersion Theory are:

1. Going outside to find the adventure around you
2. Embracing overs, unders and throughs
3. Seeking out multisensory experiences
4. Learning from taking a chance
5. Mastering the science and the art
6. Finding stillness
7. Integrating creative movement
8. Activating color therapy
9. Training in all the elements
10. Reading big books to achieve big dreams

The indispensable quality of outdoor endurance sports is the ability to immerse yourself and engage fully in the environment around you. That is why going outside to find the adventure around you is step one to practicing Immersion Theory.

Why go through the motions during your training when you could go outside and get wet, muddy, treasure hunt, run along railroad tracks, forge a river, or yes, even trespass and find an adverse entry point.

I look at working out as more than just a workout. I like my workouts to be mini adventures where I delve fully into the outside world around me, be that in the water on a wild swim in a sand pit that I ran to, on a rocky mountain bike trail, or running through native prairie grasses over my head as I explore my local waterways.

Since I was training for life, I always wanted to be training. There is no better life training than getting out in life outside. Get wet. Get muddy. Get uncomfortable. All of these things help you enjoy the life you are living by being alive. Anyone can train for a marathon or an ultrarun by running on the sidewalk or road. I make my training as fun as possible because it is always about the journey, and training is part of that, not just the destination, which might be the event you are training for.

When I trained for big goals or events like 100-mile races, I knew it was going to hurt, be hard, and I was going to suffer. Suffering was what I did on the weekends. To combat this, my goal was to build in some fun where I could, like making outside adventure runs and wild swims part of my training plans. There was plenty of fear and unknown about massive undertakings that required long months of training, travel and organization of tools and logistics. Embracing the uncertainty and the discomforts of training were opportunities for growth, adventure and immersion.

After my 100-mile ultra, when I was training for multi-day events around the world, I needed to run long and far a lot. I would run 30 miles for my long runs on many weekends in many seasons, so I wanted to get creative with my run routes. The best way to do this was to start at my house and find run routes from there. I looked at maps and trails and followed rivers and old railroad beds that had been converted to rails to trails to run in all directions from the center point of my home. As a kid, I never would have thought I would run 30 miles from my house, located between two rivers in the center of Wichita, Kansas, the largest city in the state, down back roads, trails and highways in all directions: North, South, East and West and all points in between; in all weather events: The humid heat of the summer, the sweat acting as an ultimate cleanser, the frozen icy world of winter, through the fogs and cools of fall and the damp rains of bright early spring. I started by walking out of my own front door and exploring the world around me to train.

I would often identify destinations to run to. It is always more fun to run to somewhere. These might be an arboretum or a casino (to use the 24-hour bathrooms) or a Starbucks or the confluence of a river. I always like biking to or from something better than going out for miles and miles of bike training to nowhere. Bikes are wonderful modes of wheeled transportation and I liked to use mine to get somewhere fun such as a new restaurant on the outskirts of town or a new-to me city next to mine. I built inspiring, interesting routes and learned my native land and city better. I connected with my home state by biking down country gravel roads surrounded by blue skies, green wheat and golden prairie sun, my favorite Kanas color palette. When those skies turned to rolling grey storm clouds, I liked the colors of Kansas even better with the increased energy of a Kansas thunderstorm brewing above. Walking, running and being on a bike bring you closer to the earth than you get being in your car. The world seems bigger when walking around in it. I made discoveries and had adventures along the way.

I would much rather have an experience outside in the elements, and run, bike or swim to something and through something, which is why going outside to find the adventure around you by getting wet, muddy and uncomfortable is the first step of practicing Immersion Theory.

Overs, Unders & Throughs

Practicing Immersion Theory also required me to be prepared for overs, unders and throughs. When taking to the wilds of the lands around me, I sometimes had to jump over or crawl under a few fences, or box culverts, especially when urbex urban exploring through forgotten overgrown areas of town and down drainage canals. Whatever the environment called for, I wanted to be ready to go.

By taking my environment in stride, like a parkour athlete, I found creeks to cross, walls to scale, barbed wire fences to hop, hills to power up, sand to tread through, and wild animals to sight. You find all this when you go out; when you seek out ways to run over, under and through rather than straight down a road. When you get up and show up, exciting things happen!

One winter training day in 27-degree temperatures, I decided to cross two ominous rivers in 33-degree water at their confluence. By doing this in the middle of a long, 30-mile training run, I learned that I could do it without freezing, getting frostbite or hypothermia. You hear never to get wet in the cold, but this was part of my training, so I made a calculated risk to try it. Living an adventurous life is often about calculating the proper risk. I made a decision to test myself and apply the What Makes You Test. On this day, my risk paid off, as I discovered the sloshing water was not all that cold after all! By testing running through cold waters mid-run, I learned that if I kept running and moving, my feet didn't freeze like they sometimes do in the cold, and I dried off and warmed up with my body heat. Knowing that I had crossed two flowing rivers on a cold winter day later helped me when it came time to cross a melting glacier in a whiteout in Iceland, and keep running through a foreign, other-planetary land for seven more hours.

I went to Iceland to run the 55k/34mi mountain Laugavegur Ultra Marathon in the Landmannlugar National Park area and experience the lands of Scandinavia. The morning of race day, I woke up at 3:15 am in the always-light night of the northern climes. After a bus ride through gorgeous, giant green and black amalgamate rocks that enveloped the roadsides, the cold, wet, windy ultrarun took me on a route through the national park that takes backpackers four days to hike, stopping at what were our race checkpoints for overnight stays. I completed the cloudy, mountainous run in eight hours, part of one day, hurtling over huge rolling peaks and plateaus, across placid, barren volcanic plains, and around wet pools and roaring streams. The event began with runners in fluorescent layers of clothing and all-weather gear hiking a steep up-and-up climb single file through gushing geothermal geyser steam. The air was full of the smell of sulfur and the path below my feet was slippery with grainy volcanic silica mud and wet prehistoric rock. Visibility was zero as I crossed a melting glacier during the first third of the race, slushing in ice water up to my knees, wading among glacier chunks. I had to rely on orange flags placed every 100 yards or so to find the trail, trying to see the bright colors of the other runners in between the swirling white of steam, clouds and churning snow.

The Icelandic scenery felt like I was running in a moon-scape. It was beautiful, hard and a wild of its own. This run was a way to push myself and explore a new country; to learn about Iceland while seeing its famous waterfalls and sights; and eat as much open-faced fish and vegetable smorrebrod sandwiches as possible, after soaking in geothermal pools at every opportunity. The best thing about my wet journey to Iceland, was that I enjoyed the country by being outside in its elements at all turns. I rode Iceland's unique breed of shaggy horses with their specialized gait in the rain; I snorkeled in just-above-freezing water an insulated drysuit in between the continental plates of Europe and North America in some of the most crystal-clear water in the world. I ran hours in a whirl of landscapes and moisture, as I was drenched in the surges of a new immersive environment.

I use runs to learn the flow of new towns, cities and countries by foot. Prior to immersing myself in a bucolic setting, I first had to orientate myself to the civic state. As a warmup to race day, upon arriving in Iceland, I ran through the streets of Reykjavik, taking in the best bakeries, shops and restaurants, and checking out where the embassies and nicest hotels were located. When I travel for a race, I always schedule an acclimatizing run upon landing a day or two before an event to take in a new environment and get a feel for a landscape's hills, waters and altitude. Using a training run is one of my favorite ways to connect with a city or town.

Even on vacation, running serves as a mobile way to explore a new area and environs. In college, I ran around my school town to learn the areas and neighborhoods outside of my daily campus-based life. Running took me out of my routine and allowed me to explore. Biking or walking work for self-propelled exploring as well, but the power of the run serves to mesh even more with new surroundings, combing speed with a sense of discovery.

Another way to add fun to a long training run is to find a trail and run to its very end. I love running to the end of the road. Sometimes it is a long way, but it is rewarding to arrive.

Immersion Theory is lively; therefore, it requires prep-work. When practicing Immersion Theory it is even more important than ever to always be prepared. With advanced planning and safety precautions, such as going with a running partner, studying maps, using your GPS, having essential gear on you like extra gloves in the cold and extra water in the heat, taking plenty of food, and keeping things like a knife and phone handy for emergencies, you accomplish your goals safely, even if you have to carry a few extra things around.

Carrying a few extra things around is also good training for long hikes, backpacks, stage racing and even parenting, when multiple survival bags for the parents and the baby are de rigueur. I also like to carry enough food and water to share. If my training partners or someone I meet along a hiking trail need help, I want to be able to share my food, water, layers and supplies with them. I think of these extra items as the Good Samaritan Kit when prepping. When possible, I plan ahead and visualize my event prep needs in the days and weeks before. I pack my gear and layout my clothes in advance to keep early starts from being overwhelming and to minimize stress.

Being prepared when it comes to Immersion Theory is important because you are going to get dirty. It is going to be messy. This is what happens when you venture out into all weather. Wet shoes, towels, goggles, and all manner of effects hanging out to dry around your home are going to become normal. Mud will always need cleaned off something, from bike tires, to husky paws, to muck boots. Gloves, hats and a miscellany of jackets will take over your house. Immersion Theory isn't boring. It is raw and real. It brings us back to nature and nature is untamed. If you practice Immersion Theory, you can say goodbye to average, boring easy and clean.

Immersion Theory teaches that no matter what time of year or the weather, embracing your environment, via overs, unders and throughs, is worth it because there is nothing like being in the open for clearing your head, heart and mind.

Multisensory Experiences

Immersion Theory is also creating ways to have multisensory experiences. Step three of practicing Immersion Theory encourages us to seek out these multisensory experiences.

Multisensory experiences occur when you have to use all five of your senses: seeing, hearing, feeling, tasting and smelling. Immersion Theory even advocates activating your sixth sense to perceive danger when you are deeply immersed in a new environment, like an animal in nature, tapping into the age-old reptilian, fight or flight part of the brain. When you learn to activate and rely on these senses, you become comfortable in nature. This allows you to train for any condition, in races, and in life.

One of the truest forms, and my favorite form of Immersion Theory is swimming.

I love being in the water. I love feeling weightless and the ability to move in multiple spatial planes. The water helps my mind and body relax. Being in the water is a true, immersive experience: Going under and holding your breath; being surrounded by dark blue, green, turquoise, cerulean and cyan; inhabiting a dangerous and intriguing otherworld, yet one where humans can be at home in, if only for borrowed amounts of time.

When it comes to swimming, the immersion of the environment is built in, and it automatically qualifies as a multisensory experience. Once you are in the water, you are in. You then must use all of your senses to survive. You must taste, smell, feel and hear the water when you can't see more than a few inches ahead of your face and rely on your buried sixth sense to detect dangers.

One of my most memorable multisensory immersion experiences, one where I had to implement all of the practices used in my Immersion Theory pillar, involved swimming across one of the largest lakes in Kansas in the fog.

Kansas is not known for its access to water. Over the last 30 years, though, my family and I have learned to make the best of this by using what water we do have—rivers, sand pits, lakes, and ponds—to adventure in, on and around.

I use my two local lakes east and west from my home as places to integrate into my workouts, trainings and weekend fun. I grew up camping and boating at both, and Cheney Lake in particular, has served as a destination to run or bike to, being close, but far enough away at 25 miles, to incorporate different endurance sports trainings around, like using a run/bike combination with one person running a mile, then one biking, then switching off to go further with minimum effort and training, for however many miles are required of each.

The mythos of Cheney Lake loomed large in my head as my dad was always running, biking or windsurfing there during my childhood. It is one of the windiest lakes in the United States. I dreamed of someday too being able to do those laborious, daring sports. Since we spent so much time going there for water sports, camping, running or biking, he often talked about also swimming across Cheney Lake. Years later, after tossing the idea around, the stars aligned for calm waters, low winds, the time to devote to a mini adventure and the training under our belts required for distance swimming across a lake. We were finally going to do it! We were going to swim across Cheney Lake, the destination of my childhood.

Arriving to the lake early (we always start early) that fall Saturday, we did not anticipate a foggy morning that refused to fade. After patiently waiting, and taking the proper precautions, we decided that we could still cross the lake.

My dad would kayak next to me in the support boat that had a light on the bow and stern. In the days prior to the crossing, we had reconnoitered the area and taken a photo of the point we were aiming for on the other side of the lake. By using that photo on one bank, we were able to orientate via compass and take a bearing to get to the other side of the lake without being able to see through the fog. It was during the colder off-season and early in the day, so we knew boat traffic would be at a minimum. All the support boat had to do was stay on point and the swimmer could stay next to the boat to swim relative safely across the two-mile lake traversal.

Swimming a little over two miles across an open lake wasn't a long distance for me. The unknowns and unseens about this event made it more exciting and adrenaline-filled. It was scary at first, wading into the cool brown lake water and not being able to see anything around me. I was in a totally new dimension. If I lost the support boat, I could get disoriented fast and end up completely off course, swimming in circles or in a confused exhausted situation. I couldn't see any land in any direction or my surroundings. I could literally be anywhere in the world, I thought. I could be crossing the English Channel, for all I could see or knew. I focused on staying calm and on what I could see, feel and hear.

Since the water was brown from the sandy, mucky lake bottom, I couldn't see anything more than my hand going in the water right in front of my face. I could also see my dad's red kayak bow right in front of me. I could smell the mossy mud of the lake and the far off gas of motorboats. I could almost taste that as all of my senses were fully activated. I focused on hearing the plop of my stroke and feeling the cool waters around me on my skin. Per the guidelines of triathlon, I only wore a wetsuit in water that was cooler than 75 degrees, and more often than not, I would go without in much cooler waters. On this day, the water was somewhere between 70 and 80 degrees, so I could swim without a wetsuit and enjoy feeling the water against my skin, something I missed when coated in rubber. rubber. Since I like the water, being surrounded by it made me happy and helped me keep my mind from racing away with scary thoughts of unseen boats or giant biting mystery lake fish and at peace.

The key to open water swimming was thinking about what I could sense and feeling confidant in that.

Once I reached the other side of the lake, my dad and I switched places, with me kayaking the support boat and him swimming back, just like our run/bike switch combos of old.

I have now swam across both my local lakes, Cheney, and El Dorado, plus a few more in all manners of Kansas storms and weather conditions. I use my Kansas places, and those I encounter throughout the world, to practice Immersion Theory and live out an adventurous life. Using Immersion Theory allows you to exist fully in the moment, because you have to, and activate all of your senses, thus seeking out multisensory experiences.

Learning from Taking a Chance

My first ultrarun, a 50k, 31 miles, wasn't bad. I completed my first ultra-distance race with little additional training to my recent marathon. I felt confident running and racing in the ultra environment. I liked that there were fewer racers than big city marathons, the fact that I got to run on trails and gravel roads versus city streets of a traditional marathon, and the ultra vibe aligned more with my outlier approach of a few people gathered together to participate in something they love, rather than the crowded corporate feel of modern day marathon racing. When my dad announced that he was training for a 24-hour run, I thought, "I might as well too, since he is my usual running partner." I was once again journeying to ultra.

At the 24 The Hard Way Oklahoma Ultra Running Championships, I ran 50 miles, my next ultrarunning goal. My first thought was, "I embarked on a 24-hour run and lived to tell about it." But, it was not without its challenges. At the time I remember feeling pure pain from the waist down, but there were also some high, albeit strange points, as usual, when it came to my outside life, racing and running.

Mile 15: The tornado sirens went off. Why? We didn't know. I just kept running. I had a goal, a focus and a can-do attitude and there was no time to stop.

Mile 16: The wind sped up to 40 mph and kept blowing. "Great," I thought: A new added element of difficulty to run through.

Mile 17: It started raining. "It's too early in the race for this," I told myself, but rain, as always, in addition to the winds, served as distractions from my focus on chalking up the miles one by one.

Mile 22: I finally felt warmed up. This was a huge lesson I learned that day and for additional ultrarunning. I learned that if you have the right training and mentally focused can-do mindset, when you get to the part of a marathon where things usually fall apart and get really hard, around mile 20, in an ultra, this is the point that you will feel warmed up. It is possible to feel good and want to keep going. It takes training, practice and going through the process to build up muscle and mental memory.

Mile 31: My last distance PR of a 50k. I felt good and proud, since I had started this race as a tagalong, and I knew then that I wanted to keep going despite the winds, rain and absurdness swirling around me.

Mile 45: It got dark. I was still running. It was a long day.

Mile 50: "Woohoo!" I ran 50 miles. Who knew? Who would have thought I could run 50 miles and still be running.

Mile 56: Longest run on record! I ran 50 miles and then kept going. I found the fun—looking forward to a snack, my family or a new weather event at each loop, and I kept going. I had now experienced that I could do this; really do this ultrarunning thing. My legs could be tired. I could be tired. But I could keep running. I didn't know this about myself until I went through it.

Understanding that you *can* do it by taking a chance is the fourth step in practicing Immersion Theory. Sometimes you don't know if you can do something until you do it. I didn't know that I could take my ultrarunning to the next level, by running a 50-mile race, until I gave myself the chance and opportunity to try. By going through the process and experience of achieving a big goal, I gained knowledge, understood my potential, and what was possible. Undergoing something like that—committing to the process of getting experience—lets you immerse yourself in the surrounding conditions, like running for 50 miles, absorbing them and taking them on.

After I ran 56 miles that day, the next cool fall morning while I packed up all my gear and fuel and drove back to Kansas, I began to think that since I had accomplished 56 miles, had undergone that I could, I might try for a 100k next, since I was essentially at that distance at 62 miles. A 100k would only be a few more miles to go.

One of the main things I learned during this training period was that how you feel now will change. (In addition to the weather.) You will experience many feelings during the span of an ultra. If you felt good when you started, that will change. Equally important, if you feel bad in the moment, knowing it will change helps you keep going. You will not necessarily feel worse. You will often feel better. This is a good lesson to apply to daily life as well, during tedious workday tasks and in childrearing. How you feel now will change over time.

I learned through this mid-distance ultra race the value of accepting change. How you feel at the beginning of the race is not how you will feel in the middle or even at the end. Instead, you will feel everything.

You have to be just as strong mentally as you do physically to know this and accept it. That is the real challenge: beating the head, not the body. In my case, I turn to God for help with staying strong mentally. Spirituality has always been there for me when I get tired or need extra help to get through a trying time. Praying for strength, patience and endurance would help me through in one way or another, and the routine that develops after hours of training, helped me on the next leg of my ultrarunning and endurance sports journey, just as faith had helped me through my life up until that point.

The Science & Art

Mastering the science and art is the fifth step in practicing Immersion Theory. The science and the art both apply different sets of principles to the procedure of running, extreme sports and expeditions. By mastering the science and the art, you can be prepared on all fronts to take on your newest challenge.

The science side of Immersion Theory deals with the technical aspects of being prepared like training plans, gear, food and hydration. The science tackles the physical portion of preparedness.

The art side of Immersion Theory deals with the mental, emotional and spiritual facets of preparedness. The art aspect requires you to adapt. It asks of you a savvy of mind; a quickness to problem solve; and an adroitness of going with the flow.

In order to perform in limit-pushing big-idea undertakings, you need to find the balance of the science and the art. Oftentimes, failure occurs when the focus lies too much on either end.

In order to prepare for my 100k ultra run, I had to take the science of my running to the next level. The science of running comes into play before an event: Planning gear, fuel and calculating the perfect combination of each; water, calories, electrolytes, amino acids; headlamp, pack, Vaseline, gaiters; making a race strategy; visualization; studying the course maps and aid station points. I had to develop these skills and have them down to be successful at running longer distances.

My art of running also had to evolve. The art of running, similarly to the science, came from practice, training, repetition, trial and error and, most importantly, the heart. The art of running is what really happens on a run: Realizing that the race is all hills, so your race strategy, the one you spent the whole summer training with, goes out the window. It is hot so you want a sports drink rather than your fueling drink, so your nutrition becomes fluid rather than exact. The art of running is relaxing when your legs hurt and finessing your stride on the downhills. It is about keeping your mind on the moment and not even a minute ahead. The art of running is what gets you through a 100k. I created my art of running by adapting to the task at hand.

That task was my first 100k/62 miles outside of Tahlequah, Oklahoma, for the Pumpkin Holler Hunnerd at Eagle Bluff

Resort among the foothills of the Ozark Mountains. I have since been back to Tahlequah several times and I will never forget it. The winding, gravel country roads of the Nickel Preserve are burned into my memory.

Race day was hot for October and hilly with more elevation gain than expected. At the time, the course was advertised as flat, so no one I talked to felt prepared for the monster hills. I was happy I had some recent mountain training experience climbing Mount Rainer in the Pacific Northwest.

With a late start, my run went into the night. After battling honeybees—Bees! I was battling bees during an ultrarun, as if it were not hard enough—for drinks at the aid stations, the fall of night helped to escape the slowing sun. I would not have wanted to be out on the gravely Oklahoma back roads in the woods alone. It was dark and noisy in the trees. Little did I know I would be back the next year, doing that very thing, while escaping gunshots.

My legs took a beating, but I didn't have any mechanical issues from running other than blisters and heat rash on my feet. The hardest part of the race was mental: Not being in a hurry, or worrying about what was ahead, instead staying in the moment and that moment only.

One of the things that comes with sleep-deprivation, in-to-the-night and all-night ultrarunning, is hallucinating, or seeing visions, especially at night. This happened to me on this race. Because I had read about it before in training guides, I was prepared.

During my 100k I kept seeing broken-down buckboard wagons in the middle of the road.

Instead of focusing on seeing the finish, the next aid station, or a recognizable landmark ahead, my brain decided to see, or fill in, the road ahead with wooden wagons to ease any anxiety about being done.

Ultrarunners are crazy. The buckboard wagons are proof.

In the midst of this craziness, during the last half of my 100k ultra, I first started to think that if I trained properly, made some sacrifices, and really wanted it, I could run 100 miles.

I was thinking, believing and experiencing that I could do it. I was once again undergoing that I could.

By going through that process and mastering the science and the art sides of my running, I knew I could take my ultrarunning to the highest running goal, my ultimate What Makes You Test: Running 100 miles.

I made a goal and spent the next year training to run 100 miles.

I learned so much along the way as I used my Explorer's Mindset to invigorate my training, Outlier Tactics to get my running in day or night, hot or cold, and Immersion Theory to embrace whatever environment I was in.

Finding Stillness

One environment that we can all work to embrace when we find ourselves in it is that of stillness. Finding stillness is the sixth step in practicing Immersion Theory. Finding quiet and solitude is only getting more and more important in today's always-on world.

If you always train with music or other noise, you will miss the world you are trying to be out in. Being able to run, drive and sit in silence elevates your focus to the next level. Stillness and quiet take training, like all hard things, but it is some of the most important kind. Often, it is in the quiet when big ideas strike.

Hearing the silence of the cosmos is my secret for getting through a long run, bike or swim.

This can also feel like being in the zone or finding your flow. Finding this place of zeroed-in focus and low effort is the sweet spot in endurance training. It is a spot where your body can be at work, but your mind can be at rest to wonder, meditate, think and relax as you flow through your practiced movements.

God speaks through stillness and it is a way I have always sought and found to connect with Him. Listening and existing in the quiet take training, practice and dedication, but they are key elements to endurance mindset and mental toughness training. By learning how to connect, listen and be still emotionally and spiritually, you can set yourself up to be even stronger and more capable physically and mentally.

Before a big event it is also important to find this stillness and visualize. Plan your life, plan your week, plan your day, plan you route and plan your workout by seeing yourself go step-by-step through it. You can find problems you need to solve, things you need to pack and prepare for, and anticipate issues before they arise. It can help you stay ahead of stress and be proactive about your activities.

Visualization is a key tenant in preparing for large undertakings, be they adventures, speaking events, presentations, long projects or complicated days or processes. I start at the very beginning of a trip, going through each day of travel, touring, prepping, training and racing, and post-race recovery and the return home. I close my eyes and take myself through each day, especially race day. This helps me prepare what I am going to eat, drink, wear and need in terms of specialty gear like trekking poles, warm layers or water crossing protection. Long expeditions with more time, more sports and more equipment require even more visualization and planning. The training you put in before an event is not only physical. It is mental in the form of visualization as well. There are many things in life that you cannot prepare for, but I prepare for the ones I do know, like race routes and trails.

Sometimes I found training easier than my normal life approach of hyper-busy, multitasking, accomplishing, get-it-done feeling.

Six, seven, eight, eighteen, twenty-four hours... this is a long time to do something.

But when I thought about the millions of things I did in an eight- to nine-hour workday, it was refreshing to think that for the next few hours, the equivalent to half a day of work, a full day, a long Saturday of chores, social activities and responsibilities, all I had to do was run.

This was incredibly freeing and a great way to approach the dedication my training would require because in that moment, I only had to run.

I also found long runs therapeutic. They gave my mind a chance to still and for me to think; to be alone with myself and my thoughts. I could listen to nature and hear what it was saying. Finding stillness is an important principle of Immersion Theory, in a more passive, but equally important way.

Creative Movement

Integrating creative movement is step seven of practicing Immersion Theory. Creative movement involves finding new ways to move your body. It means you listen to your body on how it wants to move and you give it opportunities to try new movements and combinations. Creative movement taps into the mental, emotional and spiritual aspects of your being, as well as the physical aspect of moving, as it addresses a deep inside need that you manifest outside through expression of movement.

In running, this is sometimes referred to as intuitive running. Intuitive running means you listen to your body on how, when and why to run. You examine your motivations, how you feel, your sleep, your diet, your current life stressors, and not simply what you have on your calendar to accomplish running-wise that day. You listen, intuit what your body needs, and train and act accordingly.

When it comes to creative movement overall, this intuitiveness is key. Tapping into how your body wants to move applies to all movement training, in addition to running.

I have always participated in more than one sport at the same time. I became a triathlete at age seven, and its multidisciplinary approach stuck. When I swam on a competitive club team, I also ran track and cross country. In high school, I competed in several varsity sports and dance. Even when I was ultra training, I didn't run more than three times a week to prevent injury and burn out. I practiced intuitive running and I crossed trained with creative movement from other sports and fitness modes.

These different ways of moving gave me additional ways to prepare. Creative movement nourished me beyond the physical. Practicing multiples sports and multiples ways of moving made me a better athlete overall. I was more well-rounded and balanced physically, mentally, emotionally and spiritually.

Cross training and moving creatively helped minimize injuries and keep me excited about training and working out. I also used creative movement and cross training to incorporate intervals and high-intensity training.

In addition to swimming, biking, running, paddling and hiking, my creative movement cross training includes group fitness classes like weightlifting, agility, step workouts, kickboxing, bootcamp and dance. I love yoga and it pairs wonderfully with running to increase mind-body connection, flexibility and mobility. Pilates and Gyrotonic helped me even out imbalances and work through repetitive motion-induced sore spots. Stair climbing and running helped me prepare for mountains while living somewhere flat. I also add in rock climbing, obstacles, skating, tires, aerial arts, or other new fun sports as they come up. I stretch, stand up, and move around throughout the day whenever my body tells me I need it.

My goal with creative movement cross training is to find additional movement. In running, especially with the large amounts required for distance training, you move so much in one direction. Integrating other ways to move spherically keeps my mind and body engaged and healthy.

You can seek ways to flow into creative moment in your daily life and in your training. In addition to stretching and moving around though the day as your body prompts you, adventure runs are the perfect way to integrate creative movement into your training.

One Saturday morning I set out to run my usual out-and-back route along my two Arkansas Rivers. On the way back, I decided I needed an emotional burst of positivity generated by creative movement. By simply changing my route home, I created an adventure run and worked in creative movement into an already established routine. I ran up stairs, across a pedestrian bridge over the river, through rocks and along a new path. I ran along a historic route and along the origins of my town's bike trail that was paved in 1970s, picnic-table-green, seeing the only part that survives today. I ran over a dam and along another river. I passed a confluence and I ran through a museum's art garden, where I did parkour on the stone walkways, ran up more stairs, and checked out an outdoor amphitheater after running under arches and across wooden paths. Then I saw a dumpster and climbed up it to take a look for treasures inside, applying the Shopping Cart Test in action. I explored another historic structure, the town's water treatment plant, and found a secret route that only required one fence jump and a narrow run between two fences to the next meadow area I was shooting for. Then I ran on the gravel of a back alley after doing some recon and spying on an outbuilding project, until I got to my last bridge crossing where I took the wet exit route back at my first river toward home.

I still covered the same mileage, but I had so much more fun on my exploring adventure run. I burned more calories, used different muscles than only my running legs, and activated other total body muscles to jump up and climb obstacles. My mind was invigorated as I sought out the next thing to explore and run to. It didn't take any more effort than my usual route. It only took an adventurous mindset, the opportunity to move creatively and activating my sense of playfulness.

It is unfortunate that in the professional business world, creative movement is not encouraged. Because it is valuable to your spirit, and at work you might spend weekdays contained and limited, the solution I recommend is embracing a sense of playfulness. When you break out of repetitive molds, your soul will thank you.

One of my favorite ways to find playfulness and creative movement is in the water. After lap or lake swimming, I dive down and hang out underwater. I move, stretch, flip and kick. I wear fins. I move in ways I can't on land. I do the things I did in the water as a kid, before I grew up and supposedly didn't get to do those things anymore. This non-exercise exercise helps me connect with the world around me and allows me to play uninhibited.

Taking a ballet class while ultrarunning helped me strengthen new muscles and move my body in ways that were not solely forward. I expanded my mind, body and spirit connection. I learned to move in new ways; to lengthen and extend. A Zumba dance class supplemented these movements even more in lateral ways. The important thing was that I wasn't limited by my desk job or by running. I allowed my soul to play and find the fun in exercise. Moving multidimensionally added an element of extraordinary to days that otherwise would have been ordinary.

Cross training, creative movement and seeking out ways to play will make you better and stronger, whether for life or an endurance sport. They will help you experience the world.

Color Therapy & Training

A critical principle of Immersion Theory is absorbing the natural world around you: Running through a forest grove surrounded by the deep green hues of fresh summer leaves, swimming underwater in the luxurious Mediterranean Sea seeking and craving the blue waters as you soak them in, or basking under a powdery pink sunset on the wide-open, big-sky plains of Kansas. The natural world is full of color and I use that color to help me train for life and endurance. Activating color therapy is step eight in practicing Immersion Theory.

Color therapy taps into colors, their frequencies and vibrations, and their ability to affect the mind and body. When it comes to treating ailments, colors can be shone on the body or absorbed via the eyes with colored glasses. Different colors are chosen to apply to different areas of the body based the seven chakra system, with a different color representing each section of the body. The belief is that every color seen and absorbed has some effect on the body's cells and the mind's emotions.

I study the effect color has on both my mind and body in an overall health benefit way. I apply color therapy principles to what I wear when I train or compete. I align my colors to how I feel, how my training feels and how my competitions or events feel. The use of color helps me prepare emotionally for large expeditions, travels and travails. I even apply color therapy when getting dressed for a normal day, business presentation or work travel. The principles behind color and color therapy can help you when choosing what to wear each day, each season, when dressing for business, and for sports and life training.

Color theory relates to the color wheel and the harmony of how those colors work together. I used color theory and color therapy to train for intense, demanding adventures around the globe. How a person uses their senses affects how they feel. Use sensory exploration to align how you feel—your emotions—with what colors you want to see. Your colors should harmonize with yourself—color therapy—and each other—color theory.

I first noticed the power of colors I wore when I would go through a certain color phase. For example, I would pick out purple clothes for my morning gym workouts, wear something purple to work, eat something purple, like a blueberry soup at lunch, and then also put on purple yoga pants at home in the evening as lounge wear. I might even eat out of a purple bowl or off of a purple platter. It would be a day where everything I instinctively chose came from a similar color tone, maybe not all the same hue of purple, but generally purple shades. This could also apply to wearing and choosing lots of green, blue or orange. I noticed that I would dress how I felt, whether I was consciously aware of it or not. I might not be sure what my body or emotions were telling me, but I knew that being drawn to one certain color at one certain time meant something.

I would get out my chakra map of the body to correlate where the colors I was choosing matched on my body. Was it my heart, my head or my digestive system? I am not an alternative medicine professional, but I would use the principles of color therapy as a tool to understand what my body needed on a holistic level to help me find balance in life. I figured, like all alternative therapies, this was ancient knowledge and the more I could learn, know and understand, the better I could connect with myself and the natural world. I found color therapy especially useful to feel aligned and in tune during peak training periods where I was under large amounts of physical stress.

When I was running for eight to nine hours at a time, I needed to wear something that felt comfortable tactically as well as color-wise. Going to the gym for an hour in the morning or evening, you can get away with wearing whatever is appropriate for your workout. The same goes for short runs outside or on the treadmill. But when it comes to multi-hour runs, you need to wear soothing, comfortable colors. It takes motivation, discipline and willpower to undertake a big training challenge. You might be scared or worried about how you will make it through a long run, hard training or intense, demanding workday. The colors you wear can help you train and function by helping how you feel.

I am drawn to cool colors like blacks, blues, greens, purples, grays and whites for long runs. They keep me mentally cool, relaxed and fresh, and that comes into play physically.

One day during 100-mile training, I was assessing my running short colors, and I thought, "I only need some in yellow and I will have every color." (I have a penchant for collecting one of everything in every color.) When I went shopping, I couldn't bring myself to buy anything in yellow, however. The thought made me hot and made me feel like yellow shorts on a run would make me have to go to the bathroom every mile. Yellow to me signified the sun, the heat and urine. It was not a color I wanted to wear when running and trying to avoid all of those things.

I felt the same way when I was planning my outfit for my 29-mile/Twenty-Ninth Birthday Run to Cheney Lake for post-running wild swimming and picnicking. I wanted to wear my new bright pink sports top, but the thought of a warm color next to my skin on a hot day for 6-plus hours made me feel overheated just thinking about it because pink, a derivative of red, made me feel hot and warm—the exact opposite of how I wanted to feel while running 29 miles in May in Kansas on a long blacktop road to the middle of nowhere.

Different people will have different colors that work for them. The important part is learning what those colors are and using them to your advantage. You can learn what colors work for you by paying attention to how the colors you wear make you feel. Does dressing in warm tones, such as reds, oranges and yellows warm you up or make you feel confident? Does dressing in cool tones such as blues, greens and purples soothe you or calm you down?

You can use the colors you find that work for you for whatever event you are dressing for. I wore a black and white striped swimsuit to train for my Escape From Alcatraz swim and chose an orange swim cap to keep me in the right Orange Is The New Black prison escape mode. The black and white stripes made me think of the traditional prison garb of black and white striped coveralls and my orange swim cap reminded me of the prison TV show that was popular at the time. This helped me stay excited, motivated and on-theme while training. I wore red and black on a work trip to one of the largest trade shows in Las Vegas because those were the colors of the show and dressing the part made me feel ready for the tasks ahead of me.

I also use color palettes to pack for trips and plan adventures. I pick out what colors and tones a destination makes me feel and use that to plan outfits and themes. A color palette is several colors combined together that communicate a feeling. For my adventure babymoon to Bermuda, I chose a color palette that matched the scenery of pink sand beaches, dark green pines, cool crisp crashing wave teals and a midnight blue to match the Atlantic sky.

I even like to coordinate my nail polish to my current event as part of a destination color palette. I wore a murky, tonal purple for my first marathon because that is how it made me feel color-wise, and I found it connecting mentally and physically: Hard. Dark. Neat. And Focused. For my epic rim to rim to rim trek across the Grand Canyon, I wore a bright, spring, canyon-esque shade of orange russet nail polish on my toes, with a spot of sparkle. It felt symbolic of the American Southwest canyon full of reds and golds, which in turn helped me feel ready to conquer that specific challenge.

It is empowering to know you are prepared top-to-bottom for extreme experiences in any environment and aligned color therapy-wise.

One of my favorite things to discover is a new color. The history of natural color for pigments and dyes spans the globe and is full of adventure. Throughout time people have gone to great lengths to find the perfect or most valuable color that their era dictates. I like to discover what color the activity I am participating in dictates.

Use your colors to help you achieve your goals and connect with your mind, body and spirit as people throughout centuries have done. Activating color therapy is an essential way to practice Immersion Theory.

All the Elements

When you train year-round for life and big expeditions, you have to learn how to train in all the elements of your environment. Being out in all the elements is part of Immersion Theory. Training is all the elements is step nine. In order to get properly immersed, you must be properly trained.

Running Long in the Heat

After running all summer through 100-degree days and 80-degree nights while training for my 100-mile run, I learned how to run long in the heat:

Get up early.
Sometimes very early. Try midnight. One am. Or 3 am. All interesting hours to be awake.

Run in the dark.
Time goes by faster. The night is a distraction.

Train with a friend.

Fill your hydro pack with water and ice.
If you use a water bottle, fill that with ice too.

Make it fun.
Run from nice gas station to nice gas station. Buy a cold sports drink or iced tea at each stop. Alternate the flavors. Fill your pack with more ice.

Take advantage of sprinklers.
Or, if desperate, public fountains. Use real water fountains for what I have dubbed a birdbath, a splash of water to the face, neck and arms.

Walk.
Utilize a run/walk plan.

Seek a route with shade.

Do an out-and-back course.
Or else run a loop course. Have family and friends meet you on the way for cold treats and sunscreen refills.

Make it an adventure.
Run somewhere new. Run around your city or through it. On one summer 20-miler, I ran through the mall, to cool off and to make it to the next nice gas station. Lastly, when it is all over, reward yourself with a Frappuccino.

Running Long in the Cold

Short runs in the cold are doable, if uncomfortable. With longer runs at or below freezing, you have to prepare to survive exposure. You could stay inside all winter, but Immersion Theory wants you outside, in the great outdoors.

Any running advice outlet will tell you layers are the way to run in the cold.

This will get you to about six miles in above 20-degree temps. If you need to really run long in the cold below 20 degrees (especially in Kansas where you have humidity and wind) you will need a strategy to get you through sweating in the frozen elements for multiple hours.

After an inspiring two-hour ultra training run one winter in seven degrees, here is what I suggest:

Tailwind run.
Run out and arrange for transport back, for example, have a friend or family member pick you up at your mileage destination; or better yet, meet them at a coffee shop, warm up, and have them drive you home, or drop off a vehicle before your run for a ride home. Cold wind on the face and creeping through fabrics can be brutal, especially for hours on end. This plan is even better if you have a hydration pack on to keep your back warm on the way out.

Use a route with emergency stops.
If your hydration bladder freezes and you need to buy water, winds shift unexpectedly, and you need to buy more gloves or a hat, or you just want to step inside a gas station to warm up or use the bathroom, mentally knowing you have that option a mile or less away is helpful.

Sometimes you will not have this option, so always carry a phone, money, hand-warmers and extra layers, especially if you're going to be on trails or away from civilization.

Layers are important.
For anything under 10 degrees, I run in fleece pants and a top. This wicks the sweat and is warm. I top this with a soft-shell jacket, double mittens, a neck gaiter, hat and balaclava for my face. (Having a stash of mountaineering gear to choose from helps.) My feet get cold during everything else in cold temps, so I am glad they don't when running. I use Vaseline between my toes to prevent blisters, which also helps keep in heat.

When you are out for several hours and get sweaty, that equals wet, that equals cold, so changing into a dry next-to-skin layer at your halfway point can help, as with switching to a fresh, dry pair of gloves or mitts, which I recommend. If you don't have a fancy set of running mittens, buy cotton throwaway gloves from a hardware store or gas station to toss in your running pack as an extra emergency layer. If you have money with you, you can stop on your run and buy a pair in an emergency. I don't like to go to Wal-Mart on my runs, but I stopped there to buy a hat once on a long run where the wind changed and the weather blew in fast, and I needed to gear-up to make it home safely. It was a fun challenge seeing how far the cash I had with me could go to cobble together a warm-gear outerwear ensemble. In a pinch, plastic grocery bags can be layered on hands or feet to block the wind or wet. This works in a cold bike emergency as well.

Start the run with a bounding Siberian husky.
Bonus points if you can find one who thinks below-freezing weather to be invigorating. I find this makes for a good warmup.

When it is done, heat back up with a hot drink and hot shower.
And know it could always feel colder. (See mountaineering, where your hands and feet go numb for multiple fear-inducing hours!)

Big Books & Big Dreams

When I was growing up, on weekends after swim meets, I would go to the bookstore with my parents and our family swim friends. I remember seeing the book *War and Peace* and thinking, "It is so big. How could I ever read something that long? Someday I want to read *War and Peace*."

I thought the same thing in college when my dad was reading the 20-plus *Master and Commander* book series. I thought, "Someday I want to be able to do that."

I used to think that about the Bible too. I wanted to be the kind of person who could read something so weighty.

I read all of them. I read the Bible in two different translations. They all had profound effects on my life in different ways.

When my dad decided to run 100 miles, I thought, "I don't ever want to do that. That is crazy."

But I did it. And it had a profound effect on my life, too.

Reading big books helped me achieve big dreams. That is why reading big books to achieve big dreams is the tenth step in practicing Immersion Theory.

Reading large tomes in size and theme is like training for an endurance sport. Diving into a long book takes hard work, commitment, focus and dedication. I found that working hard at reading hard books helped me work hard at taking on challenging expeditions and events.

Reading big books helped me reach my big dreams, like running 100 miles. They helped me with discipline and stick-to-it-ness. They helped me make my goals into habits. Reading the classics filled out my worldview. A classic is something that influenced your life; it is emblematic of a time and place; it changed you and your outlook, attitudes, beliefs. Books have helped me see things from a non-American perspective, particularly The Age of Discovery, and supported my knowledge and travels. One of the things I love about reading classics is that I learn so much—words, places, things, colors—compared to most contemporary readings that come down to me reading for the plot or what happens next. Being more familiar with contemporary culture, I found I invested more when I read something historically based, since I had to try harder to connect with the time period. I researched more and became more immersed.

If you want to get good at the hard stuff, like ultras and expeditions, you need to read books about suffering. Books about suffering helped me learn what the human spirit is capable of. A few that I recommend include *Sufferings in Africa*, *The Long Walk*, and *We Die Alone*. I timed each read with a trip to the general area they take place in—North Africa, Siberia, and Norway—and they helped me realize that life could be harder.

Training happens on a physical level. It also happens on a mental level. You get stronger and tougher in each area. Emotionally, you have to learn how to deal with your emotions of an event. You are going to feel conflicting thoughts and you have to practice telling your mind to supersede your body. All long runs are pilgrimages—journeys of faith. Having to rely on the support of a higher power, God in my case, to make it through hard things, like mountain runs and relationship struggles, has allowed me to get though them and helped me in my faith. I haven't been able to do any of these things alone. Going out and learning that and discovering this helped me live a full, complex life.

Just like literature, endurance sports immerse you in places you would never otherwise go physically and mentally.

Practicing Immersion Theory requires these 10 distinct steps, but by incorporating these 10 fundamental tenets, you will become a part of the world near you in multiple ways. Going outside to find the adventure around you, embracing overs, unders and throughs, and seeking out multisensory experiences integrates you into your environment. Undergoing that you can by taking a chance tests and prepares you for what you can achieve. Mastering the science and the art takes the principles of preparedness and extends them to physical, mental, emotional and spiritual aspects. Finding stillness helps you connect more deeply on emotional and spiritual levels, as does integrating creative movement and activating color therapy. Training in all the elements takes you beyond getting wet, muddy and uncomfortable, and allows you to thrive in all conditions, and finally, reading big books parallels achieving big dreams while expanding views, worlds and ways of thinking.

By adopting each of these three pillars of my life approach, developing an Explorer's Mindset, using Outlier Tactics, and practicing Immersion Theory, I hope you have found new ways to connect with nature, seek adventure, and become a confident winner physically, mentally, emotionally and spiritually. In this next section, join me as I further apply this extraordinary approach to fitness, life and training around the world.

PART II

Journey to Ultrarunning, Wild Swimming, Mountaineering, Paddling & Multisport

I have used an Explorer's Mindset, Outlier Tactics and Immersion Theory to run long, climb high, swim deep and go far from the deserts of Namibia to the jungles of Patagonia to the cloud forests of New Zealand to the mountains of Russia to the islands of Africa to the seas of Scandinavia, and all across America, as a multisport athlete. The journey of these experiences helped me adapt, succeed and win at life.

4   Ultrarunning

One year after running my 100k, I was back running 30-mile loops around Nickel Preserve for the Pumpkin Holler Hunnerd, this time running the full 100 miles. Before that year, I never would have thought I would be running 100 miles. I thought running 100 miles was crazy and ridiculous. And now, there I was. That is how life goes sometimes.

I trained devotedly for that year, hammering out long runs in the cold and heat, cross training with mountaineering, ballet, swimming and gym workouts, reading big books, and nailing down my science and art strategies.

When it came time for the actual event of running 100 miles, I was focused on my goal of Relentless Forward Movement.

I thought I would feel a lot of things during my first 100-mile race. In reality, I focused on Relentless Forward Movement no matter what. Being so mentally and physically on for nearly 30 hours straight was what was hard; through the hot day, through the dark, dark night, and through the next humid day; no break in the goal of going on and forward. Things hurt: blisters, IT bands, knees and they still hurt several days after my race.

Not to be without the weird excitement common in my running life, on the portion of the race I ran alone, at night in backwoods of Oklahoma, I heard about 10 gun shots and even met up with some other runners who were hiding in the ditch from the shooting. I just kept running. Strange things happen at night. Especially on runs!

Another interesting happening was that I carried a recipe in my running pack for 27 miles. One aid station named Mad Dog had dog biscuit snacks shaped like dog bones and stamped with the name of the station. I carried a couple with me and would break off bites moistened by the humidity at low points during my running overnight where they would instantly make me feel better. I got the recipe on the last lap and carried it during those last, short, 27 miles, distracted with the thought of making the Mad Dog biscuits again.

Aside from these brief moments of distraction, I curated the right attitude to keep going; to stay focused. My can-do attitude training helped me tune out anything that wasn't imperative to my goal, and act on moving forward.

I like to note that this ultrarun was actually 102 miles, as it is hard to get things to line up perfectly and be exact. Also, a good lesson for life, as life rarely lines up as perfectly as you plan.

To date, running 102 miles is one of the accomplishments I am most proud of. I never would have thought as a child struggling through a two-mile road race that it was humanly possible to run 100 miles. But it is. And it opened the door for so much more. Training for and running 100 miles helped me develop my life approach of an Explorer's Mindset, Outlier Tactics and Immersion Theory. It was now time to take those principles to the next level.

Crossing the Desert

On long training runs my dad and I would bring up new adventure ideas. These were the big, outlandish thoughts that we had to talk about to make real. These ideas were ones that would take us not only outside of our experience zone, but also across time zones. We would hit the zone, so to say in running, where you are focused and flowing, and we would brainstorm big ideas and inventive ways to travel, train and have fun. We lived out step one of using Outlier Tactics by always coming up with new ideas outside the normal realm of thinking.

One of these far-flung expedition ideas was stage racing and desert races, whispered about while suffering through 100-miler training, in the vein of, "Hey this is hard now, but it could be so much worse!"

I thought it all sounded insane at the time. Running with all of your food, water and gear on your back for days and marathons on end? While I liked the idea of traveling and running through exotic locales, desert stage racing seemed supernatural to me.

When my dad decided to run the Namib Desert Challenge in Namibia, I decided to join him. With my ultrarunning training system in place, this seemed like the next step in the ultra racing field. Where do you go after a 100 miler? For me, it was multi-day racing.

In the early '90s on a family trip to Colorado I explored the sand dunes of Great Sand Dunes National Park with my dad. Why not explore the sand dunes of Africa with him now?

I was going back to Africa. I had traveled to Tanzania in 2010 to climb Mount Kilimanjaro, the highest mountain in Africa and for safari. This time I was going for an international desert stage race—to a desert that was 50-80-million years old. Nestled in southwest Africa, Namibia was known for its Skeleton Coast along the Atlantic Ocean, where whale bones and shipwrecks had washed up against the sands for centuries.

You have to be brave to take on something new; something that might be outside of your realm of previous experience. When preparing for the Namib Desert Challenge I kept thinking about the Bible verse from Joshua 1:9: "Have I not commanded you? Be strong and courageous. Do not be frightened, and do not be dismayed, for the Lord your God is with you wherever you go." It encouraged me to be brave to take on a new big outlier-esque goal.

Living in Kansas, I trained for the desert during a wily winter, while amassing large amounts of specific white desert gear, like a long-sleeve, light-weight desert shirt, desert cap with a back neck protector and over-the-shoe gaiters to keep out sand.

I sewed Velcro patches on to my running shoes to attach the gaiters, as it would be hot enough in the desert to melt traditional glue. My mom had to take my running shoes to our seamstress because we needed a professional-grade sewing needle to penetrate the thick soles.

It was difficult to be in desert-training mode while enduring snowstorms at home. I hoped there was a correlation between breaking trail on my husky's snow walks and trekking through sand. I was running outside in 20 degrees, on a warm day, taking hot yoga inside at 100 degrees, and spending time in the sauna at 140 degrees. I was acclimating to all elements while trying to heat train to get my body used to working at the high cardiovascular levels the desert would demand.

The cold and hot temperatures made me think of the opposites of high and low; the mountain and the desert; two of the world's four corners. The mountain—and mountaineering—required gear. I had climbed Mount Rainer the summer before. It was now spring and I was headed to the desert. The desert—stage racing—was about carrying as little as possible. I was dealing with two extremes in addition to rainstorms, thunder, lightning, hours of being wet, soaked, drenched, windblown and cold: a full mix of adversity training.

In addition to getting a medical declaration from my doctor clearing me to run this event, I also had to plan out all of my daily nutritional needs, since I would be responsible for most of my own food during the race each day. I spent the months leading up to the race packing, prepping and analyzing specialty desert items and picking out the perfect ultrarunning pack to hold my mandatory gear like an emergency whistle, compass, signaling mirror, rehydration sachets and knife, and figure out how to transport all that across continents.

After taking one of the longest flights in the world at the time, from Atlanta, Georgia, in the USA, to Johannesburg, South Africa, I arrived in Windhoek the Namibian capital. The city was modern and organized among gorgeous green hills and giant palms. On my first morning I ate a pretzel for breakfast, a leftover influence from Namibia's German settlers, and a purple granadilla fruit, similar to the South American *grenadia*, which I had tried Peru, and known more commonly around the world as passionfruit. One of my favorite things to discover while traveling is new food, especially fruits and vegetables. I was so happy to find a Namibian specialty to add to my collection.

I spent a day before the race checking out Windhoek and resting up on the hotel terrace by the pool reading a Candace Bushnell book. I needed something easy, light and sweet to balance out the mental weight of my upcoming endurance challenge. Even among the capital city I felt like I was somewhere at the ends of the earth; somewhere I might end up when all other options proved over.

Five hours from Windhoek by bus through awe-inspiring desert vistas brought me to the Sossusvlei Desert Lodge, the base for our desert run.

One thing that was constant throughout was the pure vastness of the land I was surrounded by. Namibia is one of the least populated countries in the world. There was no ground transportation in the Sesriem Sossusvlei area, which was isolated and remote. Visitors came by chartered bus or plane. There was no easy way out. Once I was in, I was in.

Ever since the triathlons of my youth, I always got nervous at the pre-race meetings, briefings and gear checks. This time I joined runners from countries around Africa, like Malawi, Ghana and South Africa, the UK, Canada and other statesiders, including elite ultrarunning athletes. I was more jumpy and apprehensive with nervous energy than ever in the new, intimidating environment.

Before I moved into my bright orange tent, my home for the next week, I enjoyed a delicious candlelight dinner on the lodge's lush patio while getting to know my fellow racers. I ate all I could in true, last meal fashion, of local salads, sides, pastas, stir-fry, and made-to-order grilled game meats like oryx, hartebeest, springbok, and eland, surrounded by the grasses and stumpy trees as the Namibian night descended.

The Namib Desert Challenge was five days and 228 kilometers of running through the oldest desert in the world. It took me through mountains, canyons, famous landscapes and the summiting of two of the highest sand dunes on the planet. The race is known as one of the toughest footraces in the world, with five stages of high-endurance ultrarunning, where I ran roughly a marathon plus, up to 34 miles, each day.

The desert was hot.

It was like a hot yoga class that never ended.

With unrelenting heat, the multi-day run was hard and challenging. Average daily temps were 115-120 degrees Fahrenheit. I asked myself, "Why was I running in this? In the heat of the day?" At home I would never run at the hottest times of day, if I could help it. And now I was choosing to—had to. Even the direct morning sunlight was concentrated. While traveling I was reading Ultrarunning Magazine and came across a quote that said, "In ultrarunning you alternate between asking yourself why and telling yourself to keep going." That is exactly how I would summarize my five days of desert running.

The first day was 42km/26mi and included hiking, climbing and running through deep sand tracks that seemed impossible to keep going through. At times I wondered how anyone was making any forward progress. We lined up early in the dawning light of the desert and ran under the shade of the massive rocks around us while we could. I started getting comfortable with the extreme heat. Toward the end of the day, as I stood atop a sandy section I had just climbed, I looked down at the grassy, empty plain, as the tiny road below stretched out into yellow nothingness and far away mountains and thought, "I'm alone. In the desert. Running a marathon." When I went to the desert I had no plans of running the race alone. However, I always felt God was with me, in between the times I was around the other racers or the event coordinators.

After hours of running in the heat, the intensity stopped, but the heat did not. I would still have chunks of the day to fill when I needed to be eating and recovering, but it was difficult to find a spot anywhere in or around camp that was out of the sun and not burning up. My tent was too hot to be in or relax in. At one point I drug my bright yellow camping sleep pad out seeking shade under a large dead stump covered in thorns. I was unsuccessful. I was so desperate to escape the burning desert sun that I tried to find comfort from a thorny dead tree.

After dinner, once it got dark, I would have a little relief, at least from the sun, but not from the temperature—enough to actually be in my tent and start organizing all my gear for the next day. The still heat would linger as I endured until 2 am, when the temps would drop. From 2 am until 7 am, it was pleasant. Then I would wake up and start running.

I liked getting up and running each day, day after day, for five days in a row. It became routine, and I like routine. It was the fact that I was still running eight hours later that required fortitude.

I called day two the hot day. We ran 44km/27mi through track and miles and miles on the living Elim Dune. There was no shade. Just miles of yellow and orange sand and bright blue sky. I ran this day mostly alone, breaking it up with visiting at the checkpoints.

Day three was the day I had to overcome to make it through. If I could do that, then I could keep going. I was mentally spent from the challenges of the two days before and not sure I could keep going. The night before, I sat down and made plan: A plan to get through the race, the next day and the week. What else was I going to do? Stop? Go home? One competitor had already done that. He chartered a plane and left. Several had stopped and joined the crew following along and scouting in trucks. One had got near the point of renal failure, from the intensity of the heat and dehydration, and had to take a day off from the race to recover. Others were hobbling around with knee or ankle injuries. I decided that I still wanted to be out there. I still wanted to experience it: The world of Namibia and the desert's varied landscapes. So I figured out how. I would run when I could and walk when I needed to.

And I did it. I got through the day a little at a time.

My dad was able to run more with me this day and that helped me too. It was a good thing because when a hyena ate a mile marker, all of the runners got completely off course, and my dad helped us navigate back to the right direction. When us middle-of-the-packers caught up with the race leaders mid-morning, we knew something was wrong. These world-class runners were usually hours ahead of us. As everyone gathered on the track with no race directors in sight or in contact, a plan had to be made: Where were we running and how were we going to get there. Together we took bearings with a compass and found our way to the next section by a process of trial and error.

We covered endless rocky areas and bushwhacked through the wilderness, up and down steep grassy hills. The Sossusvlei Lodge staff catered our checkpoints and that always gave me a hope to run to. They were full of hospitality and inviting with iced water, iced tea and a rehydration electrolyte mixture the runners dubbed Leopard Piss.

At the end of each day I would shower in my running clothes, then change into my lounge clothes and hang my wet ones out to dry. With only one bag, we were limited on what we could bring with us, and this was the fastest option to clean up after the day's run and have as clean-as-can-be running clothes for the next day. It was an efficient process and showed me how little I really needed. Through the week I discovered that there is nothing better than an open-air desert shower. It was my favorite thing to do upon finishing each day and something I thought about—the water pouring on my face and skin—for the nine hours I was sweltering through running.

One of the features of this trip was that we were provided a gourmet meal prepared by a chef from the lodge in the evenings, unlike in some stage races where you have to carry all of your race fuel and own food. I didn't eat meat during the run so I could avoid any unfortunate digestive instances. There were plenty of fresh salads that tasted refreshing after a long, hot day.

Although one night I was still hungry when I went to bed. As I was eating almonds in my tent before falling asleep, a pack of jackals approached and stared howling a prehistoric deep howl right next to me. I love animals, but this scared me. I was separated by wild, cackling creatures by only a thin layer of tent. There was no way I was going out into the night after that! The jackals upped the ante of being in the middle of nowhere in Africa miles from civilization.

Our longest day was day four at 52km/34mi. The highlight that I looked forward to was ascending the famous Dune 45 that Namibia is known for. I would just have to run 34 miles, through unmarked land that I might be the first human to ever cross, to get there first. I ran through the huge rocky Sesriem Canyon, miles of track, roads and bushwhacking to the long, flowing blacktop road and Dune 45 where I ran up one of the highest sand dunes in the world after four days of desert running. It was a deep orange and beautiful against the azure sky.

It is possible to drive to Dune 45. Even though it was beyond challenging to get there, I was so happy I ran, through the country of Namibia to the landmark.

There was an excitement in the air on our last day. It was our short day. We only had to run 30km/18mi. It was amazing how happy, ecstatic actually, all the runners were. But, we also had to climb one of the highest sand dunes in the world: Big Daddy.

The dunes loomed against an overcast sky making the colors more morose and foreboding, but with a welcomed sense of refreshment as we neared the race's end. Once again among the deep sand dunes on all sides, I enjoyed the scenery break from dry grasses and snaking tracks. Sandy hills splayed in all directions, purple in their shadows and bright and eerie in the beams of sun.

As we approached Big Daddy, I climbed up a steep pre-dune on all fours. My hands and feet gripped the gritty, hot sand. I was one with the earth at her most ancient. I have thought of this moment often since then. I felt animalistic, scrabbling my way up the summit dune. I am lucky to have had that experience. I have since found myself literally crawling up other mountains, so it has been a good life skill to acquire.

Going up Big Daddy seemed to take a very long time to cover the massiveness of it all as I hiked up the ridgeline in the engulfing sand. Going down was its own adventure. I used the deep, sinking-down heel step I had learned on Mount Kilimanjaro the last time I was in Africa to slide down. The sound echoed from the earth as it took in my weight, deep and primeval. I will never forget that noise of the earth responding to my presence in a series of reluctant gasps. My shoes and gaiters filled with sand as I slid down a dune that is visible from space like I was skiing on my feet.

At the bottom we crossed another iconic Namibian spot, the white clay salt pan of Dead Vlei with its famous thorn trees. Once a valley, 700 years ago the sun scorched the dark black deadwood that hardened from lack of water when the area's climate changed.

We ran through more sand, our final push through the desert's one constant, and finished the five-day stage race amongst celebrations and glowing white flags signaling our completion. Finally, we could relax, laugh and chat unguardedly. Our test was over. We had come out on the other side of the furnace.

After arriving back at the lodge, my first stop was the cobalt pool. Poolside, I ordered a cold Namibian Rock Shandy made from lemonade, sparking water, bitters and ice. *Ahh...*rehydration. And all the water I could soak in through my scorched pores.

For our last dinner we were treated to an evening bush drive via an open-air 10-person safari truck and ate at a candlelight rock cropping set up in full game style to celebrate our accomplishment. This run was a rustic, off-grid experience and I met wonderful people, some who I would later see on more ultrarunning adventures around the globe.

Traversing the dunes of Namibia would not have been possible without my standout life training approach of an Explorer's Mindset, Outlier Tactics and Immersion Theory.

I was immersed in the golden glow of the land around me, running through the ancient, sometimes empty space, often alone. I explored and discovered a new part of Africa I had only recently learned about. I soaked up the culture and history. I met volunteers, coordinators, race hosts and fellow competitors from around the world. We were all now bonded for life through our shared desert experience. Employing my Outlier Tactics to train, especially adversity training, allowed me to thrive and survive in such harsh, raw conditions. Many places I had traveled to, I had always dreamed of going to. While I didn't always dream of going to Namibia. I dream of someday going back. Back to the back of beyond.

Volcanoes in Patagonia

After Namibia, I embarked on more international destination runs. One of those places was Patagonia.

I wanted to go to Patagonia for as long as I could remember. I was drawn to South America, and after a previous trip to Machu Picchu, I was longing to venture back to the southern Americas and their welcoming, inviting culture I had encountered. Additionally, ever since I watched the Eco Challenge adventure race on TV in high school, I wanted to be the kind of person who could compete in a jungle and mountain multi-day adventure race. When my dad and I found the tailored adventure race in Patagonia in the form of El Cruce, I knew it was my time to return.

El Cruce was a three-day stage race from Chile crossing into Argentina through mountains, volcanoes, snowy peaks, forests, lakes and valleys. This ultrarun took me to one of the wettest regions on earth, where I joined participants from 30 countries for the largest adventure race in South America in 2014. I was beyond excited to not only travel, but to compete in such a far-out part of the world. Little did I know that El Cruce would never truly be over, as I came to say, as effects from this journey lingered on in my life for long afterward.

The race was full of challenges, culturally and terrain-based. It was wet, rainy, muddy and rocky. I ran through water and up volcanoes. I spoke more Spanish than I had ever needed to on past travels to communicate and survive, and I met people from throughout South America and the world. Logistics for 3,000 competitors on teams and individuals racing in tandem and on different days played a huge role in the overall chaotic, immersive experience.

The event was a large regional draw and had an array of media coverage with two helicopters, three drones, 15 cameras, and more than 100 journalists from Fox Sports, C5N, Telefe, Canal 9, America, Argentina Channel 26, National Geographic Channel and Runner's World Spain.

Before my three consecutive days of running through the untamed lands of Patagonia began, I went through a lengthily check in process, perhaps foreshadowing the laissez-faire

attitudes during the race to come, but with a mound of cool
swag thrown in amongst the muddle of registering that many
international runners. I organized all of my gear into three bags:
one with my travel clothes that stayed at the host hotel, one
that I dropped off in a heap by a road to be loaded on to a bus
and delivered to our camps each night, and lastly my racing
backpack I would wear with water, training-tested running
foods, outdoor gear, emergency items and daily comfort needs.
I fueled for my next three days of racing with a late but delicious
dinner at the *colones del sur*-style hotel full of fresh green salads
and rich carbs after a long few days of traveling south. I was
nervous but excited to be in this outpost of old. I could feel the
wild and the need for self-reliance that hung in the air in my
rainy mountain host town nestled among the lakes at the bottom
tip of the world.

Race morning brought with it a bus ride deep into the foggy
malachite-colored Patagonia mountains. I lined up among the
other team runners along a black sand beach for a dramatic
start. As the horn went off, we thundered down a stage with
the drones and TV cameras buzzing around us. I ran fast in my
bright blue El Cruce racing jersey with my team name, Strong,
on the back, along the volcanic beach for several miles until
we reached a long climb ascending up to a huge mountainous
area. Once we reached the exposed portions, it began raining
and blowing heavily, making everyone soaking wet and freezing
out on the open obsidian summits. We ran 26 miles this day;
a marathon on day one, with two more days of back-to-back
running to go. I relished the parts where we ran through cool
bamboo forests. Those happy moments did nothing to mitigate

the miles of giant, muscle-zapping mud holes, though. The inherent amounts of mud slowed my progress to a long, slow, suck. I alternated nearly losing a shoe in the muck and trying not to fall face forward down in it or backward, as I plucked along the mud infused trail. Either way would leave me covered in dark, rich, black stink, as old as the hillsides surrounding me. I ran as gingerly as I could, balancing on tired legs, lightly navigating the path-wide mud pools, trying to keep pace and myself as clean as possible—and my shoes and running gaiters intact. When I encountered a steep, slippery mudslide deep in the forest, I had to descend holding on to a rope. There was no other way to pass. I continued running while slowly getting colder and colder as I trekked through the dripping wet jungle, meadows and countryside on my way to the first day's finish.

At camp one, I was wet, cold and covered in mud. It rained on me all evening, so I didn't have a chance to relax or air-dry any of my running clothes I would need to wear a version of the next day as well. I focused on cleaning muddy gear, getting on dry layers and prepping for the next run ahead. I enjoyed an outdoor meal of pastas, bread, salad and grilled gaucho steak, links and chicken. The plums and melon fruits refreshed me after a day of exertion and the hot drinks that followed dinner warmed me from the damp deluges. The classic asado meal helped me recover properly for the running to come. After organizing my effects and fueling my muscles, I went to sleep as early as I could to maximize my down time before it all began again.

Day two was logistical disarray. Due to heavy rains and the resulting mud in the racing range, the organizers had to change the planned course. I was ready to go at the scheduled time of

7:30 am, but didn't start running until five hours later after a disorienting bus ride and long amounts of waiting. Being a type-A American, I was always early, and one of the first participants to line up, making my waits and the confusion build.

Upon arriving at an open clearing, I had to clear the bus and sprint to the start, in fear of missing the race beginning. However, once I reached the lineup, everyone then had another long wait in store as we stood around, wearing out our legs, in the pattering rain. The race director told us the course would be shortened, however it ended up being the originally planned 20-plus miles, but that was never communicated to the racers. People ran out of water and food in the mix up. Disorganization reigned king. Luckily, I was prepared, by always saving a little extra of each in my pack for emergencies, but the organization tumults and short supplies added to the mental and physical toils involved in running theses long distances in the wilderness of another country. The sun came out and made me hot as the roads winded and I picked through the rocks. My favorite part was running alongside a beautiful viridian-green lake. I also liked running along a *morado* beach and in the shady spots among the trees and giant pastel hydrangeas. Other than those moments, day two was full of struggling. I reminded myself that I was there for the challenge, the scenery and the culture, and I was certainly getting that.

After finishing the run portion of day two, back in the open field, we had a pandemonium-filled three-hour bus ride to get to camp two somewhere in the middle of the mountains—with no water! After running more than 20 miles starting at mid-day! I was completely shocked there was no water for us at the finish, let alone post-race refueling foods of some kind. I could never imagine this style of event going off well at home. Racers expected to have water, facilities and food of some sort after races of this length. After the day of disorder, I luckily still had a tiny bit of water left in my hydration pack, so I was able to mete out a small amount and my last remaining energy gel to keep me from feeling the effects of dehydration on the endless bus ride to nowhere in the fast-approaching night.

When we did arrive to a rain-soaked camp after 10 pm, it was dark, storming and my bright blue domed tent was sagging and full of water. I moved as fast as my cramping legs would allow to get dry, eat dinner and prepare for the next day's run. It was a short, wet, muddy night in camp. Because the bathrooms were located about a quarter mile away from my tent, I had to spend my downtime doing even more walking in the rain, mud and dark. And there was still no water. I was about to go full capitalist and offer to buy a bottled water from the organizer tent before I used my Outlier Tactics to think differently to come up with the idea to fill up my various vessels (hydration pack, water bottles and dinner mug) with hot water from the dining tents. It only required just a little more walking back and forth, back and forth through camp. It was hard to believe I was still thirsty and dehydrated when everything else around me was sopping in wetness.

While I didn't sleep much that night, and the third day of running loomed large in my mind, I focused on calming my body to get some much needed rest and managing my physical needs to be relaxed as I could be when I was running and to stay focused on that. I knew I had the physical training. I had to work on the mentality and curating the right attitude to live in the moment, whatever it would hold.

Day three began under a blanket of fog. After waiting in the rain and enthused chanting from the South American crowd, the race started in the dark black silted volcanic mud slopping around my feet mixed with grainy sand portions along an uphill climb with low visibility. It was exciting not being able to see what was ahead of me. I knew it was a long climb up a volcano, but just like the shrouded start, an air of mystery clung to the run as I explored the unseen before me through a misty rainy dark morning somewhere between Chile and Argentina, surrounded by other runners in steep, narrow uphill portions, and then, no one at all when the trail spread out.

I didn't know what to expect from day three because there had been so many unforeseen changes to the race plan already. Everyone else I chatted with didn't know either. Would the course be shortened? Who knew? Several other racers had been on bus and van rides to nowhere as well and late to the race start even. At this point, did it really matter? I ran when I could and climbed hard up the volcano. I descended on single track through trees and killed it trail running down fast, right through the mud pits.

I think we ran about a 20k this day. I was not sure what was happening at the end, which included another bus and a border crossing. Despite being unclear where and for how much longer I was running, I sprinted into the finish to represent the U.S.A.! At the post-race festival field, I reunited with running friends from around the world and enjoyed a lunch box of rice and veggies, bread, a local cereal bar, apple-flavored sports drink and those delicious Chilean plums. I hadn't showered in three days and was totally filthy, but I was happy to have completed the bamboo jungle and volcanic mountain multi-day adventure race.

At the end of the race, we were transported back to Puerto Varas, our host town, near Puerto Montt, Chile, but the dropped off bags, however, would not arrive for two more hours. When they did arrive, I carried mine on my back to my hotel about a mile away, up and down the hilly vacation town, after three days of mountain running, on tired legs, covering nearly 100km. It was once again, not an early night, but at least I could replenish my tired body and mind in town with a delicious, one-of-a-kind Argentinean beef filet—an area must-do—fresh salads, rich country breads and savory and refreshing gelato.

El Cruce was still not over even after returning stateside, when I got my delayed checked bag from Chile and was faced with washing mud soaked, wet gear that had been sitting in Ziplocs in an international airport for several days. My shoes, mired in Chilean mud, had to be permanently disposed of.

While the race was hard and the logistics were challenging, it was fun to be part of such an elite group of competitors and an amazing, wet, wild, Patagonian running experience. I got to explore the far away land of my favorite famous explorer Ferdinand Magellan and his Magellan Straight I read about as a child and longed to go to someday. I was immersed in an area of uncultivated mountains and luxurious vegetation running through the hard elements. I will never forget deep muddy trails either. It remains the barometer for all mud-related adversity training I encounter.

An American Epic

After several international expeditions, it was time to do something classically American: running the Grand Canyon, rim to rim to rim. The Grand Canyon is one of the most popular tourist destinations in the United States due to its immensity and colored rockscape. It is also uniquely ours. The Colorado River roars through its bottom and the history is rich. It is a national park and has been home to Native Americans of the American Southwest for thousands of years. I had always wanted to travel to the Grand Canyon. I wanted to see in person something that captures the spirit of America's westward frontier. Running its length had become an ultrarunning challenge, so it seemed like the way I was going to get to this natural American monument was going to be to run it. It was a big goal; an astounding idea; a feat worthy of an epic. My run across the Grand Canyon and back would be 50 miles through a millions-of-years-old, 18-mile wide, overwhelmingly sized hole in the earth, visible from space.

While planning ways to delve into America's most famous natural landscape, at one point, my dad, some of our friends, and I had decided to run the shorter Grand Canyon rim to rim. That would have been a great distance, around 20-25 miles; enough of a challenge, but totally doable. However, there was a United States government shutdown at that time that interrupted our plans and closed the National Parks. Not wanting to wait until the north rim opened again in May, we decided to go for the full rim to rim to rim, from the south rim to north rim of the Grand Canyon and back to the south rim, on a spring weekend in April. It would be harder all around, but we had to take advantage of our timing and training and seize the moment and our momentum.

Luckily, my running mileage was already high from my other ultra run races, so I wasn't overly worried about covering the 50-mile distance of running across the Grand Canyon and then back again—the R2R2R. When undertaking anything ultra in size though, there is always a little worry: Worry about performance, worry about injury prevention and worry about ability. This time I was more concerned about the logistics; the geological terrain and the idea of running down one side, through the bottom Vishnu Schist rock, up another side, then back down, across, and up another trail. I would have to have a solid nutrition and safety plan in place to undertake this American classic, especially since one side, the north rim, would be entirely closed at the time of year we were attempting the crossing. We would have to be completely self-reliant with no hope of support or supplies from outside sources or the National Park Service, other than a private emergency evacuation helicopter for only the most life-threatening instances.

I always memorize an event's course and visualize my race plan before a competition when possible. It is part of my preparation routine and a safety precaution I feel more comfortable taking when tackling extreme events around the globe. If you are going to develop an Explorer's Mindset, use Outlier Tactics and practice Immersion Theory in life, it is always better to do so with visualization and a plan.

In my early triathlon days, I used to drive the bike course and scout out the lake swim and running routes the day before a race. For paddling, I study maps and drive through the countryside following the rivers for ranges and ideas. Do as much reconnaissance before an event or outdoor outing as you can. When traveling to back-wooded areas in foreign countries, this is harder. But I recommend preparing for what you do know beforehand and the known factors you are aware of. This can include studying the race information on websites and in race packets, reading travel logs from others who have been in the area you are adventuring in, familiarizing yourself with country, city, regions and terrain maps, plugging in local emergency numbers or apps on your phone, and always caring a paper version, even better if you waterproof it first, for when internet and cell service fail. You never know when and what information might come in handy especially when you are in the backcountry and you want to be equipped to handle an emergency. I also read survival and outdoor books about the area I am traveling for added resilience reserves. By reading books that relate to my current undertaking, I create built-in multilateral personal development in my adventures.

For several months before our Grand Canyon trek I worked with my traveling companions to plan our route, what to wear, what packs and trekking poles to use, where to stay, how to train and what emergency options were available to us. It helped that my father had participated in hiking and adventure trips in the area, as well as our other teammates, and had studied the region via books, maps and trips for years.

After flying to Arizona—and loading up on water that I always promised myself I would do if I were driving through the desert that no one ever did enough of in the movies I watched as a child—we scouted the canyon the night before our run, taking in its swatches of striped colors the Southwest United States is known for: desert greens and canyon reds; burnt sienna among the pines—as we reviewed our morning routes and familiarized ourselves with the general area. We dined in the westward pioneer style stone visitor's center decked out in its National Park brown and green on veggie burgers, in an Americana restaurant that reminded me of the family vacations in young adult novels I had read as a kid, and always wanted to be part of. Vacationing to the Grand Canyon is part of being an American family. Camping in national parks is part of our outdoor heritage and I wanted to be a part of that. Being at the visitor center that night among the international tourists made me feel part of American history, past and present.

The next desert morning started in the chilly dark as my mom drove our team of five packed into a rented minivan to the trailhead of the South Kiabab Trail on the south rim. We ran down our first side of the canyon with our jackets, gloves and headlamps as the sun rose to the roaring Colorado River. At first light I was looking forward to seeing the deep-seated green and intoxicating color of the river; it was my focal point while carefully picking a trail through the rocks in the dark that required high levels of mental work to sight and tread efficiently.

Once at the bottom, we ran through the varying landscapes, rocks and canyon curves, the tall walls rising beside us. As the light came up, the day warmed and running started to get tougher as the temperatures rose on the canyon floor. Like all desert climates, we were dealing with extremes: Cold temperatures on the top rims at our starts and finishes, and hot temperatures, which the Park Service warns campers about, on the canyon floor. I had to pack the right balance to stay warm, cool and fueled through the long day, but not too much to impede my running. It was a hard balance to find.

As we reached the north rim vertical ascent we were dealing with water shortages, due to some of the camp pumps being off since we were there before the high summer season. We were all prepared, but we had to ration out our supplies to stay safe. These logistical aspects were part of the challenge of the R2R2R: being prepared, but still being able to fastpack versus carrying the gear of the overnight backpackers who attempt hiking the canyon.

Twenty-one plus miles later I had hiked back up the Grand Canyon and was on the deserted north rim. At this point, I needed a desperate regrouping from the intense, hot, vertical climbing back up into the trees. It was steep and challenging, especially with a running backpack full of layers and limiting my water intake to save some for later and real emergencies. I was so desperate in fact that I passed the time imagining that if someone would have been there, at the closed north rim with a car, I would have been happy to jump in, no questions asked. I had cash on me and I would have parted with it in an instant in exchange for a ride back to the comforts of inside. However, since the north rim is completely closed with no access that time of year, there were no other options but to get it together, manage the water situation, and get back down. I used a special tool from my Outlier Tactics arsenal that I normally avoid during ultra runs: A combat nap. Lying down, visualizing and resting my body helped me get back up and keep going. I usually avoid stopping for too long, sitting down or sleeping during ultra runs, but this situation called for a serious mental and physical refocus, so I used what I learned about being on a 24-hour clock and took a combat nap break to prepare myself to descend back into the Grand Canyon, cross it, and climb back out again.

As I headed down the trail, the five of us spread out over the next section with a plan of meeting back up on the canyon floor. I once again found myself alone, doing an incredibly hard thing—running across the Grand Canyon—in a huge expansive place. I didn't feel unsafe, as we had a plan, but some of the ancient overhangs along the trail were eerie and full of echoes. One member of our team was having severe dehydration issues, and I started worrying that the emergency rescue helicopter I heard flying in and landing could be for that teammate. I had to stay mentally present to not allow my feelings or emotions affect my run or ability to reach the rendezvous.

Several hours after going down later, I was overjoyed that a water pump was on and we could all fill and hydrate as much as our containers could hold. I was also relieved to find that the helicopter hired in had not been for one of us. I said a prayer for its unfortunate occupant. To make this final regroup point even better, the National Park restrooms of the Grand Canyon felt luxurious, after being so many places around the world with no or terrible facilities, like the El Cruce run and Mount Elbrus, I was so thankful to be in America at this moment.

We made our way through a narrow canyon area known as The Box with the goal of getting to the iconic Phantom Ranch camp at the bottom of the most popular trail to the visitor's center that we would take back up—a different trail than the one we descended that morning, but still located on the south rim. Up until this point I felt if not strong, then capable; It was long going, but I was still going and in good spirits emotionally.

Once we reached Phantom Ranch, the hardest part was ascending seven miles back up via the Bright Angel Trail to the visitor's center on the south rim. It was very slow-going, steep and seemed to take for-ev-er. I would think I had gone at least three miles and I would have only gone a half-mile. Night descended and I had grown sick of all of my running snacks and was once again running low on fuel and water. I had never felt like so little forward movement was happening on a climb. I struggled on with my head down imagining lying down on the side of the trail and curling up in my emergency bivy blanket. Then the thought of how cold and uncomfortable that would remind me that I could keep going to make it back to civilization. I was tired, but not that tired.

I climbed up the trail and finished my American epic across the Grand Canyon and back again! I ascended from the deep ravine back at the visitor's center where my mom met us with the van, to transport each of us to our overnight accommodations. It was a long day that ended in exhaustion, and elation, in the dark, just as it began.

Being in the desert and with limited water supply, made it difficult to stay hydrated enough and to eat enough to meet the caloric demands imposed upon my body by this journey. Our full run/trek/fastpack ended up being about 50 miles due to some route additions to meet our trailhead at the start. Growing up, friends and books were always going on family vacations to the Grand Canyon. I was happy to get to do so myself with my mom and dad for a classic American family trip.

The trek was hard. They all are. But it wasn't all suffering. I made it fun by making the trip about more than only the adventure of traversing the canyon. It was about doing something in my own country, in the American West, land of adventures and explorers, with my family and friends. It was about pushing my limits, but also about exploring somewhere I had always wanted to go. This journey was a vacation too, so after the climb, my parents and I headed back to Scottsdale, Arizona, for specialized rest and relaxation to round out the trip even more with some of my favorite treats only available back in civilization.

My first punch item in specialized rest and relaxation always includes finding water and getting in, per Immersion Theory. I had been immersed in desert rockcroppings for the previous few days and was in need of the liquids of water to balance me out. In this case, the nearest water was at my hotel where I relaxed poolside in an outdoor courtyard and used the hot tub for water recovery therapy to expand my aching, tight calves from all the climbing.

I also implemented my travel snacks how-to guide.

I always travel with a solid stock of snacks. Travel can throw one's eating schedule off with meager breakfasts, late lunches and missed dinners. I suggest steady snacking to keep the blood sugars in check and to help avoid any lack-of-food meltdowns when on vacation and expedition.

But who wants to eat the same energy bars one eats all the time at home, or during the racing portion of one's travel, especially when one of the most fun things about traveling is sampling the local cuisine?

Since I have a penchant for baked goods, and you could say my travel life has been one long quest for cookies (getting "some good cookies" is referenced in my fist travel journal from age eight—whether this is nature or nurture is still to be determined.) I buy a couple of cookies, brownies, a cupcake or another sweet from a local bakery (or since no one does baked items like America, packaged digestives in several varieties from a grocery store when abroad) and carry them with me throughout non-racing days as snacks.

It is a convenient way to try new things, stay satisfied and even save calories, because I am snacking on the stuff I really care about between meals. And I always have my stowaway almonds in case I get in protein deficit.

Fueling and nutrition are always important, but even more so when you are adventure traveling and need to perform.

On this trip, I stocked up on my favorite Scottsdale cookies before the run to use as driving snacks, and afterward, I refueled with an array of my favorite local foods like Southwestern Tex-Mex meals, fresh green juices, iced tea and cupcakes from the places I can only go when I travel.

After adding in destination shopping, I found ways to reward myself while training, traveling and recovering that made the overall experience worthwhile.

The best thing is, I can implement my travel snacking principle anywhere I go, whether it is across town for errands or across the ocean.

The travel snack-how-to-guide, seeking out destination attractions to take advantage of, and creating specialized rest and relaxation are a different ways of practicing Immersion

Theory, but they are still Immersion Theory. I used these things to engage in the environment around me and used it to my advantage to help me find the fun to keep going.

Traversing the Island

I spent 2015 reading the 21-book nautical history series *Master and Commander* (plus its accompanying materials, of course). I had so much fun reading the novels, connecting with the characters, and traveling the world by wooden frigate during the turn of the 19th century Napoleonic Wars, that I decided my family and I needed to travel to several of the locales mentioned in the books that I hadn't yet been to. The year shaped into an Aubrey-Maturin inspired one overall in the form of exploration and adventure.

People ask me how I come up with places to travel to for runs and events. I have always felt that ideas start adding up that pull me toward a certain place; ideas and mentions in books, shows, casual conversations or articles. One of those places in 2015 was the Canary Islands.

When I thought of the Canary Islands, I thought of a stopover for colonial explorers on their way from Europe to the Americas. The Canary Islands are one of those places that everyone has heard of, but, as referenced in several novels, Agatha Christie's for one, are hard to locate. I liked this air of unknown. This would be the perfect unique island travel destination for me, especially with my interest in the famous explorers of old, sea sagas and even better, Jack Aubrey and Stephen Maturin travel there in *Master and Commander Book X: The Far Side of the World*.

I was excited when I found the Transgrancanaria ultrarun that would give me an event to train for and a justifiable reason to embark to las Canarias. The Transgrancanaria race would take runners across the island of Grand Canaria, one of the most populous islands in the Canaria chain. I liked the idea of running across an island, and seeing a continent in miniature in reference to the array of landscapes included in one crossing.

The more I researched the Canary Islands and the race, the more the Canarias appealed to me because of their exotic locale off the coast of Morocco and the Sahara Desert in the Atlantic Ocean. They also offered me maritime, seafaring and colonial history that I could explore, tour and learn about while traveling, and they were Spanish-speaking, as part of Spain, so I could practice my Spanish. I found a resort that I could stay in with my parents for a nice, easily accessible family vacation that wouldn't be overwhelming with travel logistics like many of my other expeditions. Today the islands are a popular vacation spot for Brits and other Europeans, like the Caribbean is for Americans, so there were plenty of resort options near our race site to choose one that had the best options of my favorite Spanish and Latin foods and opportunities for me to try new special island ones.

To align with my current training, I chose the 44km/27mi distance for my North Face Transgrancanaria run across the island of Grand Canary. This distance was the sustainable option for a flatland-trained Kansan at the time, and it gave me a way to enjoy my vacation without being overly worried about how to cover an extreme distance in volcanic mountains. It has always been difficult to get enough terrain training in Kansas to be prepared for mountainous races. I had learned that by finding the right balance, I could have fun, take in a new culture and suffer just enough. Plus, I was already tackling 4,000 feet in elevation gain at this just-over-a-marathon distance, and after my Grand Canyon sufferfest of 5,000 feet of gain, I knew this choice would offer plenty of a challenge.

My mom, dad and I arrived to a calmingly massive resort in the Meloneras area of Grand Canaria against the North Atlantic. I liked the colonial-style architecture, flowing fountains, luxe patios, grand salons and Spanish flourishes that dotted the oceanside. The Canary Island archipelago is less than 60 miles away from Morocco, and geographically seemed African: dry, airy and old; while culturally the island was fully European. I liked the mix of being remote, but still continental. The remoteness made me feel like the race location was a world apart from the continent of Europe or Africa, and the continental aspect was like getting the best parts of European culture, without the heat, cold or crowds. I soaked in the balmy air, walked along the sandy waterfront beach, explored the promenade, and toured Las Palmas, a city that dates from 1478. It felt old, compact and breezy.

After checking in, attending the race expo, and eating an alfresco pre-run athlete's meal, I organized to board a bus the next morning at a meeting point near my resort that would take us to the historic volcanic Roque Nublo park in the mountains of the island to start the race.

As I navigated the crowded mountain bathrooms, I lined up to start in the pine trees among an international crowd, with energizing music playing on the race's big speakers to get us hyped and ready to run.

The race began with steep single-file climbing uphill. Then it mixed in intense, pounding, rocky downhill. I mentally broke the distance down into each section between aid stations to get through the hard parts. I learned that paring down a big idea that seemed impossibly hard into doable portions gave me short, small mini goals to work toward.

As I came into the first aid station, my legs were already shaky and worn out, after only seven miles and more than 20 to go. I knew I would need to supplement my own fuel, so I sucked down as many orange wedges as I could and stuck with those in addition to my own fuel plan through the race. I will forever remember the pure taste of those oranges. I devoured them like a starving, desperate person. In that moment, I was. I moved fast and didn't stop at all, leaving speedily to go back uphill through a small town with winding cobbled streets back to the trail.

The route was green and hazy with sands blowing in from the nearby Sahara. As it got hotter later in the day, I continued on, traversing swiftly and efficiently, despite the atmosphere, over rocky trails in a variety shapes, sizes and textures. One competitor described it as a gazillion rocks with a tendency to eat up participants. I had to agree that all manner of rocks were present in full.

There was so much technical downhill that was mentally challenging as well as physically because I had to focus so much. The middle nine miles were the hardest. At one point someone in front of me was being removed from the race in a stretcher. It was not the first stretcher I saw that day. There were also lots of falls and the medical tents seemed to always be packed.

One thing I was eternally grateful for on this run was that our race numbers had our course map printed upside down, so

I could look down while running and see what was coming next. While I had the racecourse visually in my mind from studying it before, this got to be helpful when I was begging for a terrain change. Mountain miles are deceptive because you can't see them; desert miles are deceptive because you can. That is one thing I like about mountain trails. While a road marathon would have seemed like a smooth dessert, at least trail running was full of variety.

I ran at my own pace and pushed my speed. It seemed like all of the hardest parts of runs and adventures of my past combined on this one: Running alone, climbing up volcanic mountains, navigating down steep, rocky and dangerous sections, adapting my fueling plan, knowing when to push hard and when to sprint on the downhills like I learned long ago in high school cross country. I was thankful for all of my past experience to know how to break my race into manageable chunks and how to keep going even when I got tired. By being strong physically, mentally, emotionally and spiritually, I got through the last 12 miles. And those juicy, messy, delicious Valencia orange wedges; they saved me. I grabbed eight at the last aid station after throwing a cup of water on my head, one of my favorite things to do to recharge during hot races. I felt like I could finish the race strong and running hard.

That is, until the very last 1.5km where we had to run through sand—at the very end of one of the hardest races I had ever done. I ran along the promenade full of locals and tourists out enjoying the foggy afternoon, an overheated, tired, sweaty, exhausted, but determined mess. I ran through the sand of the beach while everyone else was enjoying the view, I was only focused on passing the male competitors walking in front of me. I knew I could do it. I knew I was tough. It killed my legs and took every last ounce of willpower that I had, but I ran it in, through the sand, sprinting to the finish, passing men and women along the way.

I was happy with my run, but I paid for it with very sore torn up muscles that made getting around after the race a continuation of the challenge. But after pushing myself, I knew what I had—preparedness from past ultraruns, focus on the task at hand, and at the end, true grit. I learned that I could run far in the mountains to my max, and I was thankful for the opportunity to use all of the skills and talents I had acquired following my life approach of developing an Explorer's Mindset, using Outlier Tactics and practicing Immersion Theory leading up to the Transgrancanaria race. I had now been immersed in a new thing: hazy desert sand wind from the largest hot desert in the world.

After the race as I hobbled around the stairs and outdoor walkways along the promenade, I enjoyed the most amazing food inspired by the Mediterranean and the tuna migration routes of the Atlantic. In addition to authentic Spanish and Canary Islands specialties, fresh fruits and veggies were available in full, which is always a rarity while traveling, so I could refuel in style.

My sore legs were thankful for the resort's many pools and the thalasso, seawater therapy, spa that included a hydrotherapy pool, an anti-gravity saltwater pool, steam baths with aroma, sound and chromo (color) therapy elements, crystal and herbal integrations, a sauna, ice room, and several other sensory experiences that almost made up for the painful remnants of my run.

Even after the Transgrancarnaria race, I craved Valencia oranges and the color orange. I sought it out in clothing, jewelry and food, activating what my body was calling for in terms of color therapy to help it heal.

If it were not for developing and living out my Explorer's Mindset of discovery, adventure and freedom, I might never have traveled to a maritime explorer's nook of the world for this Spanish island crossing. I used Outlier Tactics to train and compete in this high-level endurance event and Immersion Theory to accept my environment, thrive despite it and recover.

Antipodal Full Circle

In January 1996 my mom, dad and I traveled to Australia on a two-week vacation to the summery southern hemisphere. Twenty years later, In January 2016 we again embarked for two weeks in the Antipodes, this time to New Zealand for the Tarawera Ultramarathon.

The Tarawera Ultramarathon was in the same race series as my previous Transgrancanaria run. By competing in this additional race in the Ultra-Trail World Tour grouping, I would get to travel to another new country for an ultra on the continent of Oceania. Plus, I had always wanted to travel by campervan, especially to a British Commonwealth, and New Zealand is set up to encourage touring this way. By traveling from the South Island to the North Island via van, I would get to explore much of the country by driving and camping in its outdoors. I would also get to absorb its culture and run through large parts of its landscapes, around lakes, through forests and past waterfalls for total immersion into the natural elements.

Each leg of our journey had a distinct feel, from a guesthouse in the outdoorsy, adventure-based mountain town of Queenstown, to camping on the sparsely populated wild West Coast under the Southern Alps, to a huge suite with a dining room bigger than the entire campervan in downtown Wellington by the quay, to a motor lodge in Rotorua as our running base, back to a beach town in the Bay of Plenty, and finally a high-rise hotel in Auckland's central business district.

New Zealand was expansive and full of greens, blues and sun. My color packing palette revolved around these tones of tropical light in turn. I loved Queenstown's lakefront beach area and mountain-town vibe. I tried flat whites, classic ginger slices and black currant tea among huge trees and explored the sediment-rich rivers, lakes, sounds and straights by boat, air, gondola and runs to keep my legs fresh for my upcoming race.

In the rainforest we camped and enjoyed Anzac biscuits and passionfruit desserts like Pavlova under the nearby Southern Alps Mountains and their snow-capped peaks. I watched the sun set on the beach on the West Coast and the Tasman Sea, feeling like I was in the warm and tropical South Pacific. I was glad I had picked up a bag of local kumara chips before we started the road trip portion of our journey, as there weren't many dining or gas options along the way or other places to amass provisions. My travel snack manifesto of buying the local favors to snack on in between long intervals common for travel meals was coming in handy once again.

From the South Island, we crossed the Cook Straight via ferry to Wellington on the North Island where we toured the harbor, botanical gardens and the city's history, while I dined on crumpets from cute breakfast cafes. We then drove to Rotoura, a volcanic region full of geysers and a center for native New Zealand Maori culture, for the Tarawera Ultramarathon run.

My dad and I joined 400 international athletes plus locals for the 60k/37mi ultra that was closer to 40 miles of running by the time it was all said and done. Since we had wheels of our own, we could take our time orientating to the city and the forests around us to better understand the navigation of the race. We were able to drive to the race start the day before to get the lay of the land to help visualize and plan for the run ahead of us. After checking out the historic bathhouse in the drizzling rain and dining on a veggie tart and passionfruit ice cream, it was time to rein in the touring and focus on my New Zealand ultrarun.

Having the camper van at the race start might have made it one of the most comfortable pre-race experiences, as I felt cozy and warm in the spacious inside awaiting the start of the race. However, I was nervous, as always, with my anticipation keeping me on high alert, and soon found myself lining up with the other runners from around the world in the cool, dark and rainy morning for the start of the race.

As the event began, I could see the lights of runners moving through the New Zealand forest single track in the misty dark. I felt alive and excited to be part of the international ultrarunning community once again.

I broke up the 40 miles of this race by running to each aid station and using those checkpoints as mental milestones, my usual tactic when they are identified before an event. I had memorized and scouted the racecourse and terrain beforehand, so I could rely solidly on my visualization plan. The checkpoints were well-staffed and efficient, and we could even leave a drop bag at one in the middle for extra food and race necessities mid-race.

The first 10 miles of the run went well. I was getting warmed up in the light rain on the rolling hills with lots of mud and sliding that necessitated me staying engaged and focused on not falling or slipping off the trail. This proved a good mental distraction. The next four and 10 miles brought so much climbing or running uphill and lots of solid downhill that I could fly on as the tree canopy enclosed me in its green flesh. The middle six miles were the hardest. It was just after the 24-mile aid station and halfway point that the trail miles went on forever. It started to get hot and humid. The thickness in the air reminded me that I was running through tropical forest and made me thankful for the cool rain of the morning that had kept the heat at bay up until that point. Had I needed to run longer in the heat and humidity, the run would have been much more challenging. The good part about these miles was the conversations I had with other runners on the trail. Talking with runners from New Zealand helped me connect with the spirit of the country and ultrarunning—I could feel the freedom of being out in the wild, but I was with other crazy, self-motivated like-minded individuals to keep the loneliness and emotions of mental solitude at bay. The last eight miles were hard, as the forest trail continued to wind and the rain started up again in a torrent, but that was the point where I knew I could get the run done, as I could trust in all the eight miles I had run before and rely on my training and past experiences in training and racing to finish. The fact that it started raining hard again eventually helped revive me.

The thought of running alone for 40 miles was not appealing to me at the start of this race, but the moments where I was alone on the trail, without any other runners nearby or in sight, were actually my favorites. I could fully focus on silver ferns and New Zealand elements around me, as I got more comfortable being one with the living vegetation. Once I could put the suffering I was undergoing by running for nine hours aside mentally, I could relax in my emotional solitude. This is something I could only learn by training and experience. It helped me in this race and has helped me in life as well to complete long, arduous tasks and responsibilities. I had been working for so long already, why not continue and go on? I remembered to relax my mind and body and accept my journey. I had taken on adversity and combated the stresses of life to get to this run in Oceania. Running through it all gave me the persistence to complete it. I finished the Tarawera Ultramarathon in the wet rain, soaked through but happy, content and at one with the forest.

The run was hard, but not any harder than my other races. Ultrarunning requires as much or even more mental than physical work. It takes mental work to stay in the moment and solve each problem as it comes. It takes mental work for the mind to supersede the body to keep going and stay positive. This race was not as technical and rocky as Transgrancanaria, but it was still full of tree roots, with lots of up and downs, large amounts of climbing, and slippery from the mud, but not as muddy as El Cruce.

At the finish I grabbed a hot cross bun and a local plum from the racer's tent and then went down to the drop bag area and got in the Tarawera Falls waterfall and river. Even though I was soaked and it was raining among the misty trees, it was important for me to get in the water, as the race information promised finishers could do after the event. I longed for the weightlessness I would feel. I had been focusing on that for more than 10 hours as my reward. I clamored down the bank into the cold river where a strong current pushed back against me. Despite the waters threatening to wash me downstream, the river was refreshing and I was able to stretch all my aching muscles and stabilizers out, even if I got a few strange looks from the others around me. I was in the water getting my full immersion therapy and it was worth all the risks and running it took to get me to that point in the middle of a cloud forest on the North Island of New Zealand in the South Seas.

I then changed into warm dry clothes in a unisex trailer for runners to re-robe in and we waited on my dad to finish, while still standing around in the pouring rain and continuing to get water and mud everywhere.

An important thing to remember and train for is that these races do not end when the run stops. We were still miles from civilization. That is why in my planning and visualization, I always prepare for after the race as well and have food, water, extra clothes and a transport plan when I can. I do this so that I can recover as easily as possible when I am in an already exhausted state. Being prepared for the after portion of an event is part of having an Explorer's Mindset because you are looking beyond the horizon of only the finish. You look ahead to be prepared and equipped. As I learned in mountaineering, you have to also get back down the mountain. In the case of expeditions, you have to be prepared to also get home. In ultrarunning, this meant I had to get back to whatever I was calling home base at the moment, feed and water myself, and generally not fall apart when I was pushed to my limits. Many times for me, this also meant pushed to the limits of my patience. Endurance is often about boiled down patience. The mental training of staying on task and on focus was also part of my ultra journey, as well as staying patient.

After walking several more miles to the car and to collect all of our various drop bags, through tested, wet patience, we had a 50-plus mile drive back to town where we had left the vehicles. But thanks to our international ultrarunning friends who were in country to do the race too, we all got to ride together in their car and not have to wait on the main bus transportation. I was still damp, crammed, cramped and tired, but I was among family and friends who had gone through the trial of the run as well, so we could bond over recapping the race and basking in our tired, shared silence.

The next morning, I celebrated with *two* New Zealand Frappuccinos. (I didn't want to miss my chance to try the local flavors.) There were so many more New Zealand adrenaline activities I wanted to do, while we were there, like a childhood dream of bungee jumping, but I had to prioritize the 40-mile trail run, which was its own extreme sport. I had spent more than a year talking, planning and training for it. In addition to the mileage I had to run to efficiently race a 40-mile trail run in another hemisphere, I also worked on planning the best possible trip with the resources I had available.

The long-distance run training I had put into this trip helped me find resilience in times of crisis. The New Zealand trip served as a reward, a point to focus on and make it through to. I dealt with pain, loss and suffering through run training, even when that training meant suffering of an additional physical kind. Having the Tarawera run to train for and look forward to made me stronger and helped me overcome the personal life trials I had been handed. Learning to think of my emotions as temporary helped me through the hard times. Having a positive, can-do attitude in life, as well as in running, and being patient were all lessons I learned through ultra.

After the race, as I recovered, I snapped a photo of a checkout ad at a fast-casual ramen shop on the quay. I like art and logo styles that incorporate symbols. As my mom and I were standing there, we recognized many of the symbols, and were happy that they had all been a part of our New Zealand trip in some way or were going to be soon.

That is what makes a trip successful: Learning, trying, doing, seeing, watching, and tasting iconic parts of a new culture. By focusing on more than a race or a run, I could be a true global citizen by participating in new cultures. These activities are part of approaching life with an Explorer's Mindset as you discover and journey through a new way of living.

From *jandals* to rugby to gum boots to cricket to moas to manuka honey and more, the fact that I could identify all of New

Zealand's top cultural symbols meant our travel experience was top-notch.

When Life Gets Hard... RUN

Running is the best life metaphor. Just because the road is closed, does not mean there are not other ways to go forward. When you develop an Explorer's Mindset—seeking out discovery—use Outlier Tactics—particularly adverse entry—and practice Immersion Theory—like embracing overs, unders and throughs—you can always find a way to move ahead.

When life has gotten tough, training for a run, swim event or mountain has helped me find another focus and outlet.

During hard times, like in runs and expeditions, I try and remember that I have to live in the moment. This is often said. By taking this maxim a step further and focusing on making each day, as it comes, my focus, I have been able to tackle challenges of many kinds and deal successfully with adversity as it comes, using adversity training from my Outlier Tactics pillar.

The sad, sick (and by sad and sick I actually mean pretty cool) thing about ultrarunning is that it does not matter that I have not been sleeping, am exhausted, am sick, have been overwhelmingly busy, and have to get up early tomorrow. I know I can run the long miles I have scheduled. Because I have lived through this; this was my 100 miler training alarm schedule with settings at 1 am, 2 am, 3 am, 4 am, etc., et al. This training schedule taught me that I can do it. I just have to keep going. One thing at a time. One step at a time. Making each day my focus.

I was able to get through the other tough parts of my life that involved pain, suffering and loss because I had turned goals into habits. What started as a goal to run for an hour on Saturdays, like I had when I was home from rowing during college, became a weekly goal, a training goal, and then just part of my life as the miles grew and grew. Creating this habit of running any time, any place made everything else in my life manageable because I had learned how to get up and run through almost anything. I was able to continue my running routine through the hard times of my life because I had run so much it became routine. The routine made it manageable and manageable to keep going. I was constantly putting myself on the line and creating new ways to administer the What Makes You Test as an Outlier Tactic.

The repetition of my habit made the habit doable. I trained often enough on certain trails that I learned the local wildlife that lived nearby. I knew on one section of the river where I paddled there was a single white duckling that lived among the gray geese. I learned where the mean ganders lived on my run, but befriended them anyway. I found where to locate the beaver's den on my bike route and when best to spot eagles and owls among the trees along my sandy river trails. Running was hard, but I created my own real life Disney movie full of local animal friends to distract and entertain me, and enjoy the life happening around me more fully, as I practiced Immersion Theory.

Finding the Sweet

When you are running and training hard, or going through challenging times of any kind, you need to find the sweet stuff. Becoming familiar with the local animals was an example of this for me. When you are pushing yourself physically and mentally, it helps to give yourself rewards to look forward to. These are your emotional rewards. Having something to look forward to is one of the secrets to winning at life. You have to find, via your Explorer's Mindset, the sweet stuff. I call these somethings to look forward to the sweet stuff.

The sweet stuff can be an event or a get together with a friend. It can be a family celebration or planning a trip. It can be trying a new food or sport. More simply it can be a reality TV show, binge watching a period drama, pop music you love to sing, or cookies, lattes or another desert of your choice. The sweet stuff can also be those still moments of happiness in your day that are good. It could be a walk with your dog in the early morning gloaming or golden hour of the evening. It can be soaking in the hot tub after a swim or the steam room after a workout. It can be applying your favorite essential oil that makes you feel happy and alive or relaxed and soothed. The sweet stuff can be small things, but it is always the little moments that pace the big moments; the things that make up an ordinary day. Spiritually speaking, the sweet stuff can be the blessings you see in your life, big or small: A fuchsia sunset, a fluffy puppy, a cuddly baby or the miracle of making it to work on time.

In between century bikes rides, working toward ultra belt buckles, paddling in all manner of watercraft and multisport training, I traveled to easy and sweet destinations like LA, Palm Springs and the Bahamas, to swim with dolphins. I peppered my endurance sports life with girl's trips full of quality easy time and the indulgences of plenty. When I would return home from hardscrabble challenges on the other side of the world, I would once again celebrate living in the land of giant iced drinks by carrying as much iced water with me as possible. My life wasn't all training. It was full of a mix of multilateral personal development and finding the sweet to balance out the hard.

One of the ways I actively find the sweet stuff is water. I seek out water. One of the best ways to recover from the week and a long, sweaty run is *thalasso*, or saltwater therapy. The at-home version of this is a pool plop or hot tub soak. This can also be found at the downtown YMCA pool, a mountain lake, the South Carolina seashore or the river on your run route.

I love being in water, and have always found it therapeutic to mind, body and soul.

During stressful times, a desert run for example, I crave it. I remember fantasizing about the plunge pool at the lodge in Namibia. The first thing I did after completing that desert race was to go get in that pool. It had motivated me for five days straight.

During deep times of stress, nothing has felt better than diving under and feeling the freedom of another dimension.

I found getting into the water particularly helpful postpartum, a traditional time of very deep stress. Being in the water, either swimming, or playing and floating around helped me get back to me and reconnect with my non-pregnant body. I used creative movement, part of practicing Immersion Theory, during postpartum and post racing to celebrate being alive. Creative movement is an essential part of being human. Finding ways to move and being in the water is one way to reward yourself within the framework of your daily life, especially if it is hard.

During hard times, find your own emotional rewards to look forward to. The good thing about the sweet stuff is that it is individually determined. The trick is making time to determine it.

You have to seek it out just like you do discovery, adventure and freedom. You have to curate what works for you, just like you do with a can-do attitude. Discovering your own sweet stuff is a way to build multilateral personal development, as you learn your motivations and what makes you happy and fulfilled. Ultimately, it is a way to always be treasure hunting, as you hunt for your sweet.

Running through the hard times and finding the water helped me tackle life challenges. If running taught me resilience to face the hardships of life, then water taught me ways to escape.

5   Wild Swimming

Quiet. Peaceful. Eerie. Alone.
 The warm water feels soothing compared to the jarring temperatures and added hostility of cold waters, but you better play it safe or you are going to get yourself into trouble quick, as the darkness makes the alien environment more disorienting.

You are night swimming.

I often think about mountaineering when I am open water or wild swimming. Especially the alpine, midnight, start of a big summit climb when I am dark swimming and alone with my thoughts in the water.

Both endurance sports make you feel like a guest in nature—like you don't belong in such wild settings, and that you better keep your wits about you to survive.

Fording & Diving in Open Water

Despite the wild dangers of waters fluid or frozen, if you are a swimmer, the water will call you. It will ask you to come in and discover it.

It might invite you to get up early and celebrate the summer solstice. Your summer comes to life by watching the start of its dawn from nature's view. The black waters part as you stroke through the living deep, the sun rises in your sight line and you greet the start of the longest day of the year.

The water might call you in middle of winter. Maybe you haven't been to the pool in a while, and you aren't training for anything, but, suddenly, your muscles will crave the water and the lengthening effects of a swim workout, and you absolutely must go.

It might be on the first warmish day before spring when you can think of nothing but taking your husky to play in the river. He loves the water and you love it too, even if it is not the cleanest. It is a prairie river full of whim. You can never stay out of it. It is part of you. You grew up on the river. You ford the waters stopping at the sandbars under the bridge. Being in the water no matter what is the most natural thing for you and him.

It also might happen in summer: On a lake, in a boat, when you can no longer stand being above rather than in. You jump up, throw off your towel, and dive. You have to explore the water.

Practicing Immersion Theory is one of the key pillars in my standout life training approach. Being immersed in the element of water allows you to explore a new world. Marathon distance swimming takes that to an additional level.

If you want to be a successful marathon swimmer, you have to be comfortable being alone in your own head.

Open water swimming is lonely, more so than running. You are totally in your own world.

This is why distance runners might be focused, but distance swimmers are more so. There are fewer distractions from the outside world. The mind has to be at peace with itself. It is all it has in the water. Finding stillness is even more important.

Like mountaineering and distance running, the world of open water swimming is full of adventure opportunities.

I used swimming as a world travel opportunity, inspiration and a new way to explore. If I once dreamed about climbing the mountainous Seven Summits, the highest mountain on each of the seven continents of the world, when I got into the world of open water and wild swimming, I expanded my sports view to think about also one day swimming the Ocean's Seven, a marathon swimming challenge of swimming seven of the world's famous channels, like the Cook Straight in New Zealand, akin to the Seven Summits of mountaineering.

If the world is 70 percent water, I learned that we as a human race have so much more to discover and do.

Swimming the Hellespont

One of those discoveries was swimming the Dardanelles Straight crossing open water from the continent of Europe to Asia.

In order to swim across the Hellespont in the country of Turkey, as the area and swim crossing are known, I had to take on more distance swimming than I ever had in the past for club swimming or triathlons. I trained for this challenge in my favorite Kansas sand pit lakes by swimming across and around their perimeters. This in itself was an implementation of an Outlier Tactic. How audacious to train for a world swimming event in Kansas sand pits. I would learn that distance ocean swimming was vastly different than flatwater swimming. I had to go from a landlocked lake to the wilds of the ocean.

I didn't have ocean currents to train with, but by training in all manner of Kansas wind and weather—training in all the elements per Immersion Theory—I was able to have waves and water chop to lend credence to my water training. I had swam in the ocean many times growing up and on all of my travels, so I was not totally unfamiliar with its currents and impulses. But for my training, I used what I had around me.

I also learned to go longer, with fewer rest breaks. I worked on focusing my mind and relaxing my body. I had fewer distractions from the world around me, like running offered, when I was swimming. I could feel the water, I could listen to it, I could even taste and smell it, but I couldn't see much. I had to learn to be deeply inside my own head and to be at peace with that.

I found the stillness and relied on the multisensory experience happening around me to succeed.

I stayed motivated during my training for the Hellespont crossing because I was taking on a swim made famous by epic poetry and heroic adventure. In mythology, Leander would swim nightly to his love Hero across this stretch of water, and the romantic poet Lord Byron became the first known person to swim the Hellespont in 1810.

I was excited to travel to Byzantium and again to my beloved ultramarine blue Aegean Sea I had fallen in love with one summer in Greece. I was going to the Middle East, to Istanbul, to the crossroads of East meets West. I would be swimming this very crossing while soaking in the flavors of that ancient land and center of commerce, history and stories of the ages.

More than 500 swimmers, with 175 foreigners from 22 countries, in addition to the Turkish participants competed with me in the 2013 Dardanelles crossing. The straight was closed to shipping traffic for a short time during the Turkish Victory Day swim event each year.

After arriving in country and traveling to the racing site, I visited with the other swimmers from around the globe and took in the mix of cultures that combined at once in Turkey. I heard the muezzin calls for prayers at the pre-race events and had dinner under the glowing blue light of the minarets. The crescent moon and star of the scarlet and white Turkish flag greeted us as it did the Ottomans centuries ago.

During a practice swim the day prior to the race, the waters were welcoming and calm, the complete opposite of race day. I had my first hot Turkish tea in matching mini glass cup and saucer outside on a pavilion and walked along the Canakkale promenade by the historic Trojan horse of the nearby site of ancient Troy. I took in a traditional Turkish breakfast of honey-comb, apricot and cherry juices, cheeses and simit breads, and explored the Turkish bathhouse and outside pool terraces at my hotel, as I stared across the wide straight at the classic blue waters I would be swimming through the next morning.

I woke up early in the dark and traveled to the meet up point via bus with my dad, who was also competing in the swim, and the other swimmers from our hotel, including a few American movie stars! Famous people always seemed to be hovering around my family's adventure travel world. After stripping down to our swimsuits on the Asian side of the straight and leaving our post-swim belongings in checked plastic shopping bags at the finish, I joined the hundreds of other competitors to board busses and ferries to cross to the European side, where we would start our swim by running down a beach. It was disarming to only have my swim cap, my goggles, and myself, as I rode on a packed bus and ferry to essentially the other side of the world. I had no money, no phone and no water for keeping hydrated. It was only me and my ability to get myself across a three-mile stretch of ocean in a foreign country between two continents.

Traveling across the straight on the ferry I relaxed my mind and body to preserve energy for the unknowns of my upcoming swim. In the event's 10-year history, the day of my swim brought the worst conditions yet, with record high waves and winds, I would later discover.

The race started and I ran down the beach to swim about a 5k through high wind, waves, strong currents and multiple patches of jellyfish.

The ocean felt cool and refreshing at the beginning as I stayed strong staring at masses of jellyfish floating just below me. There could be sharks and other sea creatures out in the open too, but I didn't allow my mind to think about those distractions. Just like in lake swimming, it was easy for the mind to get carried away with unknowns and the dangers of the deep. I was practiced at keeping these thoughts at bay, but they tried to jut up in the massive ocean just like the waves ahead of me. As I got father out to one of the first buoys, I had to battle a killer current where as hard as I swam, as hard as I kicked, every time I looked up to sight my swimming line, I was going nowhere. It was so disheartening. I started to worry about the whole swim. Would I run out of energy? Could I beat this current? Could I make it through? There was a support boat nearby and lots of other swimmers struggling through the bottleneck point near the start, so I took heart, put my head down, said a prayer to God, and plowed forward as hard as I could to get away from the current and properly navigate the reminder of my swim.

After the half-an-hour current episode, the large swells made sighting, navigating and efficiently swimming a challenge. I had to constantly sight the landmarks on the Asian side of the straight to make sure I was swimming in the proper direction. The waves were so big I had to work hard to see above their swaying. There was a large arch I had to make about mid-way through the swim, that if I missed, I would get caught in a current that would take me out to sea, past the Mediterranean and down to Syria. The event organizers had stressed this fact at our pre-swim navigation briefing and it made me apprehensive and drove home how important choosing an accurate individual course was on the swim.

Once I made the turn, I felt like I could relax, but I still had to stay on point to not overshoot the finish area. During this third portion of the race, I started to think that out of all the competitors, nearly 700 people swimming at the same time, and 20 or so support boats, I wasn't sure how I ended up being completely alone in the waters. I looked around, below and above and there was no one near me. I could see boats and other swimmers far away, but I knew they were too far to help me in an emergency. I was all alone in the waters of an ocean between two continental worlds. I was lonely. I stared to get tired and I felt like finishing this event, and surviving, was totally up to me. I was the only one who could get myself safely out of the endless ocean. I had only a swimsuit on my body and no food, only the energy reserves within me and my own physical, mental, emotional and spiritual strength. The only thing to do in that type of situation for me was to start praying for safety, calm and the power to keep going. I put the loneliness aside and focused on swimming, one stroke at a time.

As the nautical flags of the marina on the Asian side came into view, and got closer and closer, all I was thinking as I emerged from the waters, climbing the finish ramp, on shaky legs, after swimming most of the race completely alone, was, "I made it out of there!" The water felt like a foreign land; it wanted me out; I was not welcome; it was a fight for life and survival. As much as I love the water, this event drove home the fact that I was a guest in nature.

I stared back across the gleam of the sapphire Hellespont at sunset that night, knowing I had crossed this famous waterway by my own propulsion. There are certain places you love instantly and take in fully in the moment. There are others that seep, settle and change you without you realizing it until much after the fact. I had always wanted to go to the Holy Land and the Levant. During that thrilling, scary swim, where I prayed to make it out alive, I found myself making a pilgrimage of faith of my own.

Turkey is a county that when looking back, totally changed and broadened my worldview. In addition to touring the major sights of Istanbul, tasting Turkish coffee and visiting the Hagia Sophia, somewhere I had wanted to go since high school history class, swimming the Hellespont allowed me to learn about a new part of the world by being immersed right in the middle of it.

I used my Explorer's Mindset to explore a new-to-me area of the world, read books about it, study its history and taste its flavors. I used Outlier Tactics as I trained from Kansas with what I had around me—a form of wind, waves and water—for an international swimming event. I relied on all six of my senses as I swam through the aquarelle blue waters of the Dardanelles, staying strong and focused physically, mentally, emotionally and spiritually, and practiced my Immersion Theory in all the elements.

Cold Water & The Baltic Sea

When training for triathlons, I would typically plunge into my first lake swim of the season in the spring on May 1st to prepare for my summer racing schedule. The water would be cold, but with a wetsuit, not unmanageable. I could then swim outdoors in open water through the fall of October until the Kansas waters got too cold again and winter froze over.

When I learned about a new endurance sport born in Sweden and Norway that combined my love for running, swimming, ultraruns and marathon swims, I was keen to try it.

Swimruns, as this new combo is called, were becoming popular in the seas of Scandinavia and the mountain lakes of Switzerland. This new sport combined my two favorite triathlon elements—swimming and running—while leaving out my least favorite of the three, biking. I had done plenty of aquathons growing up, in college, and as training for my triathlons. An aquathon is a swim run race with transitions between the two. In an aquathon you might run three miles, have a transition, swim a mile, have a transition, and then run another three miles. In the new swimrun, there were no transitions in between the two. I would alternate running and swimming, going from water to trail in one fluid movement, often for ultra-like distances and times, through and across chains of islands in cold-water climates. It was a whole new sport in a whole new world.

If I was seeking something out of the ordinary, swimruns were it. It was my newest endurance sport discovery. But first I needed to learn how to swim in colder water. Luckily, on my last trip to the lands of the North, I had snorkeled in Iceland in just-above-freezing water in a special insulated dry wetsuit like my polar explorer young adult heroes. I was ready to adapt to my next challenge. I wanted to advance my open water skills and take my wild swimming to a new level.

After using swimruns as a training novelty on the weekends, my dad talked me into entering a swimrun race in Stockholm, Sweden, raising the stakes on this new adventure sport. The new mode of swimrun required research and training.

There was an entire system unique to the sport of cutting up a specialized, thinner and more maneuverable wetsuit to make it wearable for running, attaching pull buoys to my legs and paddles on my hands, and running in all of this, plus my swim cap, goggles, hydration system and nutrition that I had to learn, study and train with, in addition to the physical fitness training in swimming and running. Since there were no transitions between the two sports, I would swim in all of this gear, including shoes, for middle-to-long distances, like a half-marathon run, between open water swimming bouts. One of my first steps in new gear and new sport testing was to buy special tailored-for-wet-environments shoes out of Sweden.

I had swam in running shoes before, like during water crossings on adventure races, and it was challenging. But my new specialty water shoes worked remarkably well, and helped train me to be able to swim more clothed in the future, something I consider a survival skill and one I was happy to have. As I swam more in cold open water, with my new shoes on, I had no trouble swimming with them or my extra swimrun gear. I learned to feel like I was running in the water.

After investing in my own specialty wetsuit also from Sweden, and the remainder of the necessary tailored gear, it became time to brave the cold water for swim/run repeat training intervals at my Kansas lake. I would soon be swimming in the Baltic Sea along the coast of Sweden. I had always wanted to go to Sweden and see the Baltic Sea, but I never dreamed I would be swimming through it.

For my cold water swims at home that spring, I wore a rubber swim cap, a silicone swim cap, and a neoprene skull cap in low temperatures for my own three-layer cap system that I learned is de riguer in the world of UK-cold water swimming. All the gear, on my feet, body, head and attached to my legs and hands, left me feeling like I was a part of an aqueous military operation, especially as I would emerge out of the water, clamor up steep banks, and start running through the trees in my newest ensemble, practicing my Outlier Tactics and Immersion Theory, while exploring this new sport. I was ahead-of-the-curve, participating in an out-of-the-ordinary endeavor as I ran in and out of the water in a suburban neighborhood in Kansas, training soon to dunk myself in Sweden's Baltic waters.

The lake water was cold during my training, but I knew it could always feel cooler. The more I swam in it the more I adapted. That first head-down dip was always so shocking! I would swim on instinct only for the first five minutes until my mind calmed down and accepted that yes, my face and hands were freezing, but it was going to be okay.

"Just swim," I told myself. Yes, my kick was weird because I was swimming in socks and shoes.

"Just swim," I thought. Yes, the whole thing is a bit bizarre, but…

"Just swim," because it is fun to be doing something different, enjoying nature and experiencing its elements, be they rain, wind, cold water, whitecaps, whitehorses or waves, and using Outlier Tactics and practicing Immersion Theory.

After a few ins and outs of the water, I warmed up and my muscles felt good. I got hot running, then cold swimming, and then I would equilibrate all around. I topped off my cold workouts with a hot shower, a cozy sweatshirt, and a Frappuccino, and enjoyed the rest of the cloudy, rainy spring Sundays with a good book and a warm homemade dinner for a full mix of hot, cold and in between.

I kept up my adaptation training as race day got closer, building out my kit and acquiring gear. I swam more and more in the windy, wavy, green waters in water temperatures of 50 degrees and air temps that were similar. I kept my running miles up, adding in swim training at the pool for distance and speed. I would also run to my local indoor pool, swim, then run home for brick workouts, which were one of my favorite ways to spend Sunday afternoons in the springtime. I have always loved the combination of running and swimming.

The more I practiced swimrunning, I felt like a true water adventure, as I ran from water to land in a stealth, streamlined manner. Plus, this sport was natural progression from triathlons, ultras and marathon swims for me, and a way to expand my travel opportunities and endurance sport repertoire in sports that I knew I was already amenable to.

As the Stockholm trip approached, I read Nordic books, planned a packing color palette full of modern tones echoing the white nights of summer, organized what sights to see and researched what foods to eat while there. The island-to-island race was structured with teams of two, and my dad and I signed up as a mixed team. My mom joined us on this trip to visit family friends who were living in Sweden at the time.

The 21km/13mi of trail running and 4km/2.5mi of open water swimming for the Stockholm SwimRun event began on a Saturday afternoon, at the warmest part of the day, in a centrally located meadow in the city. We were running through the Stockholm Archipelago that is made up of tens of thousands of islands. We ate a fresh, healthy, pre-race meal of noodles and veggies. After waiting around for several hours and the race meeting, it was time to start piling on the gear for the late race start at 2 pm Not knowing what the weather would be on race day, we waited until the event to cut our wetsuits off to make it easier to run it, but still keep us insulated from the chilled water. Everyone else seemed to have that idea too, as the last hour before the race had all teams breaking out their scissors and nervously cutting up their expensive custom suits. It was a warm day for that part of the world, so even though the lowest water temps would be cold in the 50s, we made the right decision of cutting the suits for the trade off of maximum mobility on the runs.

About 300 teams raced in the event. As an international team, we were interviewed before the race by one of the organizers. It was awesome to have our support crew of my mom and family friends out to keep us company at the start and finish and cheer us on during the race, a rare thing for hard-to-get-to, remote international events I usually competed in.

Our race included nine swims ranging from 1500 to 50 meters with runs in between ranging from one to three miles. While each of these distances are short sprints in themselves, doing so many for four plus hours made it a tough middle distance pacing event: not short enough to sprint, but not long enough to go at a slower distance pace.

The race started with a fast mile run. I was warm with my wetsuit, nerves and adrenaline pumping, so getting into the first 50-degree water felt good and refreshing, if cold! My face, hands and feet were icy during my whole swim, with my feet staying numb through the first run on the gray rocks and trails through the serene trees, the second swim and the entire second run. So much was happening, so fast, with so many people swimming, it was hard for me to take it all in. We swam past sailboats, yachts, into a narrow area with a nice pushing current and then into more shallow, reedy water that was warmer at the surface, which was a welcome relief. I exited one swim in the midst of cattails before running on a winding waterside trail. I will always remember the distinct rounded gray rocks that define Sweden's coastline.

I enjoyed navigating and swimming to something. I couldn't see very much as the water was dark gray and I had to keep my dad within 10 meters of me as part of the race rules. The mental distractions of all I had to think about and keep track of, with my supplies, teammate, and dicing the entries and exits on slick rocks and cold waters, were helpful in taking my focus off my freezing feet and hands.

The middle swims were warmer, except for my fourth one, which was chilling across a wide-open water body. I got so cold as I swam through the seas of the archipelago, I was thrilled to exit the water and clamor up and over a concrete dam in my wetsuit, shoes, pull buoy, hand paddles and hydro pack as a change of pace and to warm my body up. The runs took us through parkland, including sheep pens we had to close behind us as they belonged to the Swedish Royal Family. It was a sunny day, so people were out enjoying the island parks, open areas and structures, which entertained me on the winding, weaving, rolling runs. I am sure the racers kept them entertained as well, in our aqua gear outfits of neoprene. I even saw a husky, playing in the water no less, which is always a good luck sign for me.

The last few swims were back in the cold body of water that we started in. It always felt invigorating though and got me ready to run again.

The swimming was fun, cold and subsumed me, as I took in the landscapes, trails and varying waters. The running was running, so it was hard. I wanted to run and swim faster, but I had to pace myself for the event that took several hours to complete to not run out of fuel, water or muscle energy, not knowing how much of each the race would take. Despite the physical challenges and hardships of exiting in and out of the water and navigating the under and above surface worlds, I enjoyed taking in the sights, the boats, the lands, the rocks and the people around me during the race.

After finishing, changing, enjoying another catered post-race meal of latkes and vegetables, we walked back through the parkland and took the metro to our hotel. It was a nice break being so near civilization, but yet still submersed in something utterly wild. I rewarded myself with a liter of cold water and an intriguing pistachio, marzipan, chocolate Swedish desert. It was different but delicious—kind of the perfect capstone for the international swimrun event.

One of the things I liked most about Stockholm was the coffee house culture and all of the fresh, healthy food options. *Fika*, the Swedish tradition of having an afternoon coffee and sweet break, is one of my favorite things now, too, especially with a *kanelbulle*—a Swedish cinnamon roll—or the cardamon version—*kardemummabulle*.

While in country, I had a fun time reading about the Royal Family and visiting their palaces. I was even there for a royal wedding. The actual wedding was taking place during the SwimRun event, so I was thrilled to participate in the practice procession the day before. It was all part of soaking in the world around me, and practicing Immersion Theory, either in the Baltic Sea or the old town of Glama Stan, by accepting and being at home in all environments I found myself in.

Escape From Alcatraz

I learned to focus on my long swims training for the Hellespont. I had conquered my fear of swimming in cold water in Stockholm swimming in the Baltic Sea. Could I take on my fear of swimming with sharks? Could I survive being immersed in the environment of sea lions, seals, and great whites in the famous bay of San Francisco? It was time to find out. Enter the Escape From Alcatraz Swim.

My knowledge from the dark and cold of night swimming and mountaineering was about to become even more real and even more useful.

In American lore, the Alcatraz penitentiary is thought of as inescapable. As an island located in San Francisco Bay, the federal prison is known to be surrounded by cold waters, killer currents, legends and danger.

I had always been too nervous for this swim before. Could I make it? It seemed too far and too cold; the currents too strong and too dangerous.

But I had come a long way in a few short years, conquering many endurance and life challenges, and I was ready to tackle this one. I loved adverse entries, trespassing and breaking a few rules every now and then. I used Outlier Tactics like these to train already. What could be more anti-establishment, more outlier, than escaping a prison via water?

I knew that to complete the race, I would have to rely on my interdisciplinary sports training along with a little gusto. I knew to escape the inescapable I would have to apply my theories about how to win at life while using all I had learned as an endurance athlete up to this point to sight my line, swim strong and kick as hard as I could for warmth and speed. My approach of developing an Explorer's Mindset, using Outlier Tactics and practicing Immersion Theory all combined to enable me to complete this odyssey. By using my Explorer's Mindset I found a new body of water to explore, an event to compete in and an experience to try. I used my can-do attitude to take on a new challenge of cold water and fear if I had the ability to make it to shore. I felt like an outlier escaping from a famous prison and this aligned perfectly with the rogue aspects of my personality and life approach. Lastly, I would be in the water, immersed in my favorite world, albeit with sharks, and possibly, with seals and sea lions.

The Escape From Alcatraz Swim, an iconic world swimming event, ended up being two miles through 57-degree water, on a 55-degree day in San Francisco, California in the Pacific Ocean. The length of the swim varies each time due to winds and currents on any given day.

I met my follow escapees at The St. Francis Yacht Club in the Marina District during the pre-dawn hours of a Sunday morning, checked in, and got into our full-body wetsuits on the beach in the dark. We loaded into an assortment of motorboats that drove us out into the famous bay, through the wind and dawning daylight, staying warm by huddling in our neoprene and throwaway cotton work gloves.

We were going to be dropped off at Alcatraz Island, the former and notorious federal penitentiary.

I was pumped but nervous and ready to go, as I jumped off the boat, popped up against the vegetation of the island prison, as soon as possible to stay ahead of the pack of other swimmers, into that new wet world. I was full of adrenaline about hitting the frigid water and swimming two miles through the mysterious dangers to shore. I was in a new body of water discovering it with all my senses, when I could remember to make them work, in between swimming as fast as I could, while still pacing myself for the waves ahead.

In that kind of cold, you go, go, go. You don't have the time or energy to mess with thinking.

Being out in the bay in the cold water was exhilarating and fun, in a crazy, I can't believe I am here doing this way. Looking to the bay and cityscape, I liked being on the other side. It was a waterside view, from an original angle. Who gets to see the city this way? I was swimming into shore by my own propulsion through dark blue. I thought about being an escaping convict, swimming toward the buzzing city full of laughter, entertainment, fun and freedom.

The swim went well and I stayed calm and focused, happy to be in my own head, until I came closer to where the plaguing currents set in. I could see the finish, but had to work hard mentally and physically to overcome the waves holding me back, navigate the protruding rocks and make it to the safety of the solid earth once again beneath my feet. My goal was swimming forward, relaxing and feeling the water instead of the cold.

My feet were frozen solid blocks of ice upon finishing, which I anticipated thanks to mountaineering and the Stockholm SwimRun. My solution, as always, was to run. I ran up the sandy beach in my wetsuit, swim booties and swim caps, through the finish and into the meadow behind the beach. I kept running until I could slowly start to feel my feet again. The benefit from running, climbing and swimming in the cold before was that I knew if I kept moving in the warm air, the body heat I would generate would help me warm up.

On my last trip to San Francisco, I had seen swimmers and surfers in their wetsuits, staying closer to shore to catch the waves. I didn't know how I would ever be one of them, but now I was. I was the one in the water with the wetsuit. And with the seal bobbing around the finish—a true immersion experience.

I was glad I studied, learned, trained and completed this classic swimming event. I got to go back and be the kind of person I wanted to be when I was younger. In addition, I prepared by reading, watching, eating and listening to time-honored San Francisco books, movies, foods, like sourdough, in homage to San Francisco's early mining days, and music, like Third Eye Blind for modern day SF-vibes, the '60s classic "San Francisco" by Scott McKenzie for cultural context, George Strait's "Give It Away" for a heartbreak country vibe, and Fleetwood Mac's "Gypsy" on repeat, which I had in my head during my swim, powering through the velvet underground of the Golden Gate Bridge, to fully experience one of our last trips as a nuclear family and a lifetime swimming experience.

6 Mountaineering, Paddling & Multisport

In the summer of 2000, I went to Hurricane Island Outward Bound School for a two-week backpacking and canoeing adventure development trip. A group of other male and female teens and I hiked and camped through Maine and New Hampshire's North Woods and sections of the Appalachian Trail. We paddled through lake and river watersheds, culminating in whitewater training, as part of this experience-based outdoor learning and leadership program.

Naturally, it was my dad's idea to send me off to wilderness school. He was a NOLS—National Outdoor Leadership School—graduate.

Outward Bound was quite the shocking, memorable experience for my 17-year-old self. I had climbed a Colorado 14er, and hiked and camped with my family and friends since I was nine months old, but being out, surviving in the backcountry for that long was totally new.

From 50-pound packs, to 75-pound miles-long canoe portages that lasted into the night, from forming strong bonds with trip mates, to going two weeks without showering, to surviving frightening loud thunder and sheet lightning in the great outdoors miles from a structure or civilization, this trip was infinitely character shaping. I spent two days completely alone in the woods on solo with only a small amount of food to ration out, which was nothing compared to the long days hiking with my heavy pack, dragging tools like axes up mountains to help repair trails, and paddling sessions across bodies of water through mounting storms.

Despite the hardships, I would recommend this type of wilderness survival experience to all teenagers, and people in general because it makes everything else in life easier.

It also set the tone for my future life in the mountains. I practiced leave-no-trace hiking and camping. I took the proper safety and preparedness precautions. The two nights I spent alone in the woods taught me that I could survive alone. They allowed me to experience true self-reliance for the first time. I practiced staying mentally strong as I combated the fear of the woods and I learned how to stay calm in the midst of danger. I also learned to always respect nature, especially when entering the unknown.

Mount Kilimanjaro

One of those unknowns turned out to be Mount Kilimanjaro.

Ten years later in 2010, I decided I *needed* to climb Mount Kilimanjaro. Mount Kilimanjaro is the highest freestanding mountain in the world. It is also the highest mountain in Africa.

I kept seeing articles, stories or photos on the internet about the mountain. It continued coming up and asserting itself into my conscious. It was a thought, an idea, pressing for realization.

Luckily, in the years leading up to my moment of truth, my dad had become a global explorer, skiing to the north and south poles, climbing Mount Aconcagua in South America and Mount Kilimanjaro. I knew I could ask him to go again with me and teach me all things big summit climbing.

It was funny because when I was still in college and my dad brought up wanting to climb Kili, this mountain in Africa, I didn't understand why he would want to do that. But there I was a few years later, feeling the same way. It was something I needed and wanted to do. It was a way to take my endurance to the next level and see a part of the world I had always wanted a way to see.

This is how thoughts work. They are giants that seek to be realized. This can help you achieve your goals and come up with all kinds of ideas. But you also have to be careful about it because thoughts can push. You want to make sure they are good ones and worth carrying through.

While I had always traveled extensively with school, friends and family, 2010 was the start of my global adventure travel; where I would go to a destination to do an event, not just for vacation, travel or to be a tourist.

I read Hemmingway's *The Snows of Kilimanjaro* and watched movies and documentaries about Africa. I began acquiring real mountain supplies, like heavy down parkas. I needed to be prepared for cold weather and the moods of a volcanic peak. This wasn't a Colorado 14er. This was one of the Seven Summits on a continent I had always wanted to explore. I had no plans of conquering the mountain, as I would not deem that possible, as merely nature's guest in her majesty. I was interested in conquering myself though. I wanted to test if I could do it. Could I ascend this component of the Seven Summits? Could I become a real mountain climber? Did I have it in me? The only way to answer these questions I had within myself was to try.

On a family trip to Australia, my parents and I climbed Mount Kosciuszko in the Snowy Mountains, which is the highest mountain in Australia. I climbed my first mountain, Mount Yale, in Colorado two years later when I was 14 with close family friends. I had my Outward Bound training and was ready, with research and advice from those around me who had more experience, for this next summit.

In addition to anecdotal work, for Kili training I climbed several mountains in Colorado the summer before and worked on my mid-distance running. I implemented my Outlier Tactics to find ways to climb the highest mountain on the African continent from the middle of the flat state of Kansas by running stairs and using outdoor obstacle interval training. I thought differently and creatively to problem solve for our lack of mountains in Kansas, not for the first or last time. I immersed myself in all things Kilimanjaro and Tanzania, as I was so excited to go to Africa! And even better, after the climb, we were going to go on safari.

You never forget your first trip to Africa. I remember disembarking the plane in Arusha, Tanzania. It was night and the airport was small and open-aired. I stepped off the aircraft to a warm, lush, tropical outside world full of buzzing creatures. On the dark van ride I saw so many people walking along the side of the road. Everyone was walking! They had plastic bags and five-gallon buckets and there were motorcycles with two riders everywhere. This was Africa. People were out. Life was happening. We careened through the narrow dirt roads of Arusha, full of clothing shops and open butcheries, meat hanging among the flies and the car exhaust of daily life. Africa was alive in a way like nowhere else I had ever been. I was surrounded by the madness of a city at night, with its currents rushing by.

In the morning, everything around me was vibrant green: leaves, trees and grasses. It looked neon against the rufous dirt of the roads and trails and glowed in the flush of being.

In my future travels, I had come to understand that the rest of the world was more similar. People walked everywhere. They walked around the highway and the road. Shops, residences and business were built right up alongside the street. Dogs slept directly on the asphalt. It is the United States that felt different. Almost everywhere else I went, it seemed, had more of a colonial influence and was structured in a similar manner. The suburbs and ways of the United States were what felt dissimilar to me.

Our group chose the six-day Machame route to take us up the mountain, passing through five climate zones including rainforest, alpine moorland, alpine desert, volcanic lava rock and ice caps.

Kili was a busy mountain. Around 180 people with 800 porters were climbing at the time I was. One of the most challenging parts of the climb was sharing pit latrines with all these hikers. I will spare the horrifying details, but I do prefer the great outdoors when logistics permit. Little did I know then that I would end up in places much worse.

I started from Machame Gate among the travelers, hikers, guides, assistants, cooks and porters, all amassing gear, food and supplies, and hiked through the jungle's mossy vines in my daypack and hiking boots to Machame Camp for the first night.

We were well fed on our climb. We started each day with a hot beverage: water, tea, coffee, or hot chocolate options. Breakfast in the dining tent was porridge, toast with butter or peanut butter, fruit like oranges, papayas and baby bananas and eggs. Sometimes lunch was boxed for picnics, other times it was soup, pasta and bread. After climbing through cloudy, misty rainforest, we would have more hot drinks and a snack like popcorn, digestives and roasted peanuts. Dinner was vegetable soups, bread, pasta, cooked vegetables, meats and fresh fruits and veggies like avocado, cucumber and tomato. We would usually eat our meals in a tent dedicated to dining set up by our porters. It felt luxurious and echoed the images I had of African explorers of old setting up camp, but in a more approachable, modern way that wasn't exploitive.

I hiked to Shira Plateau Base Camp on day two beginning to get above the clouds. My hands were coated in dark grey grit. Everything began to get and stay very dirty from the dusty mountain. The rainbow of bright blue, yellow and red tents stood out in pops of color from the black rock of the mountainside. Each day I layered on more clothes, and brought out my gloves and stocking cap as we gained altitude.

On day three I hiked six hours to Baranco Camp where the trail was studded with dark boulders against the gray talus. After a picnic lunch we stopped at Lava Tower for an optional climb. I thought it would be a small hike up the tower, but turned out to be a very scary, unassisted, hanging-on-for-dear-life rock climb.

I was glad I was with people I trusted. I was on a total adrenaline high after that fear fest. Reading in my tent that night, I watched the orange yellow-gold sunset over the jagged dark peaks, knowing that the next day would bring one of the most challenging portions of the climb.

Day four started out with climbing the Great Baranco Wall. The photos I had seen showed climbers thrusting their bodies against a porous volcanic rock, on a narrow ridge, with a small path that went up and up scaling its way up the wall of the mountain. Scaling Baranco was fun; more cardio, less fear, but still enough to get my heart pounding. We stopped for lunch at Karanga where I had the most delicious meal of the whole trip: a grilled cheese sandwich with tomato and cucumber. It was just the right taste at just the right time and made up for the latrines not having doors. I was the only woman in our climbing group on a mountain full of male climbers and porters. This was an anxiety-inducing situation for me.

We hiked about three more hours and camped at Barafu among the piled, steep rocks. It started to get cold, and we all started to lose our appetites due to altitude. From here on, we were not able to eat much.

Day five was summit day and I started climbing at 12 am, an alpine start, and reached the summit six hours later right at daybreak.

It was dark, cold and foggy with freezing mist. The wind was harsh, and I was miserable, but I forgot it all the second I saw that iconic Summit of Kilimanjaro sign that I had seen in all those pictures that had inspired me to one day get to this point myself.

With altitude sickness setting in, it was difficult to eat while climbing to keep my strength up. I had to work hard consuming calories in order to have the energy reserves to finish the climb. The steep parts near the top required mental focus and *pole, pole* as the porters say in Swahili, slowly, slowly. At this point in my life, this last portion of the climb was one of the hardest things I had ever done.

I climbed Kilimanjaro when there was still snow at the top. Even today, the temperatures are warmer and there is less and less. We got up fast enough that it was still dark when we summited. I loved being on the rooftop of the world as the sun rose.

As it became light and the clouds lifted, it looked like we were on the moon. I saw dawn rise above the clouds surrounded my frost and a slowly appearing aquarium sky.

Then we had to get down.

It turned out I didn't like going down. I learned how to do a downhill mountain sink step to let the loose, gravely volcanic rock push me while leading with my heel. It took quad strength and I never felt quite confident or fast enough to keep up with my climbing partners. But I learned this skill on Kili that helped me get down many other volcanoes, mountains and sand dunes in the future. I didn't know how valuable this scree experience would be at the time, or that it was the start of a grand adventure to many more continents.

I hiked and sledded the loose gravel three hours back to Barafu where it was morning and the whole accent seemed like a dream. I took a fast nap and tried to eat lunch before hiking three more hours down to Mweka Camp.

On the last day we hiked a few hours down to Mweka Gate through more mossy jungle. I loved the hanging vines. There we said goodbye to our great group of guides, cook and porters and transferred back to the town of Arusha to a Safari Lodge. I wore the same shirt for five days and hadn't showered in six, so it was time.

I enjoyed the high of climbing my second of the Seven Summits by relaxing by a cold Tanzania pool and reorganized, repacked, cleaned gear and prepared for part two of the trip, my African Safari.

The first stop was Tarangire Wildlife Park via a four-door extended Land Cruiser with a pop-up top.

Elephants are my favorite animals, and to see so many at home in Africa was beyond my wildest dreams come true. We also saw giraffes, zebras, wildebeests, impalas, lions, waterbucks and birds decked out in full plumage.

I overnighted in tented lodges at the Tarangire Safari Lodge, located right in Tarangire Park with sweeping views of the Tarangire River waterhole. It was both calming and wild. I felt like I was living out a Happy Valley vision. We couldn't take any food into the tents, for fear of baboons, and something unknown chewed through my ziplocked sunscreen and dirt-stained running shoes. The food was soothing, coming off expedition staples, and the atmosphere relaxed, with dangerous undertones.

On safari day two we went for an early game drive in Tarangire and saw more animals, including more elephants, a troop of more than 100 baboons clustered around a giant baobab tree, known as the tree of life, and warthogs who reminded me of my husky Fritz at home.

After Tarangire we drove to the top of the Ngorongoro Crater, the largest unbroken caldera in the world, for a night at the Ngorongoro Wildlife Lodge.

Day three brought early morning game drives in the Ngorongoro Crater, where I saw four out of the Big Five safari game here alone: elephant, lion, rhino and cape buffalo. We didn't see any leopards, the fifth of the classic big five, but we did see cheetahs, hyenas, jackals, emus, flamingos, gazelles, monkeys, hippos, antelopes and thousands of zebras and wildebeests along the plains and waterholes.

When I arrived in Amsterdam sometime during my 42 hours of travel westward, global travel always became one long day at some point, I remember enjoying eating a hearty, solid sandwich and fresh juice. Twelve days was a long time to be on the Kili diet. There wasn't that much to buy or snack on in Africa, which seemed very different to my American ways, developed as they were in the land of consumerism's thousand-plus choices.

I returned home from Africa a new person. As it is said about the continent, it gets under your skin. My Explorer's Mindset had taken me there and I used my Outlier Tactics to train. The thing that stuck with me about Africa was that there was no other way to see it than to be immersed. That was the way to win.

The Inca Trail

Traveling to Africa and climbing Mount Kilimanjaro allowed me to explore a new culture in a ground floor, fluid, living way. Not long after I returned home, I was at a mountain film festival back in Wichita with a feature on Machu Picchu. I remember sitting there with a group of adventure friends thinking, "We should do it again. We should go to Machu Picchu this time."

It was a similar type of trip, with porters, cooks, tents and daily hikes that was doable with my current training schedule, and I had a group of people interested in going with me.

In high school my Spanish teacher had a poster of Machu Picchu in the Andes Mountains in her office. I would stare at it and think, one day, I am going there. I knew it was high altitude and challenging. I knew it was far away and hard to get to. I dreamed about someday having the skill, opportunity and ability to go there. And with the help of my dad and some friends, I went. It was the most rewarding thing to fulfill a young adult dream.

Peru was beautiful. It is one of the prettiest places I have ever been. I loved the architecture, the culture, the history and the huge, luscious green mountains towering in all directions.

I prepared for the trip by practicing my Spanish, creating colonial, military and artisan sartorial themes, and reading and watching South American classics.

I flew through Lima and stayed a short night in the Gran Hotel Bolivar, where Hemmingway also stayed, to our base town of Cusco high among the mountains of Peru.

The rainbow is an emblem of the Incan Dynasty and a symbol for the city of Cusco. We spent a few days before our hike, shopping, walking around the city, visiting the Sacred Valley area and its markets, exploring Incan ruins, getting to know the native lambs and llamas of the Cusco area, and spotting a few good-luck rainbows.

We toured the temple of the Sun, once the center of the Incan Empire. Spanish colonial buildings were built on top of ancient Inca walls and terra cotta roofs lined the green hillsides around the city below crisp blue skies rich with rain clouds.

As we acclimatized for our upcoming trek, we stayed in a renovated 18th-centrury manor house with luxe courtyards, patios and balconies, and drank cups of the famous coca tea to help us with the altitude in the salons, richly decorated with 18th-century Cusco School paintings and surviving colonial frescoes.

Our four-day, three-night climb was a moderate expedition overall, although we reached 13,000 feet at some points. Going up the high rocky steps of the winding Inca Trail was a cardio rush. Going down the giant stone steps, I felt a deep respect for how the Incas built such a long, complex trail. Some of the stones were so big, I almost had to jump between them. It was truly a jungle mystery and giant work of art. The trail spiraled through the vibrant hillsides and peaks as we hiked in rain jackets and ponchos to escape the ever-present dismantling rain. We camped each night among the alive-greens and ancient sites. Under the cover of night, I slept in my yellow tent among mounds of wet hiking clothes as we crested closer to the skies, weaving in and out of the 26-mile hike, on one of the most famous trails in the world.

The food served on my trek and in the city was amazing, from classic Peruvian chicken, to new Andean cuisine, with brightly colored new fruits and vegetables, including a South American staple, the yucca, which we ate warmed and like a potato.

On the last day of our hike through the buzzing jungle, we descended into Machu Picchu, a 600-year-old masterpiece, only rediscovered again in 1911, after a drenching rainstorm. We headed to the Sun Gate for the best view of the renowned city. As the clouds lifted, I was grateful for the warm drying heat of the sun after being wet for four days. I became enchanted with the roaring power of the Urubamba River far below. I could hear it rushing 1,000 feet up the jungle trail, reminding me of its presence at the start of the Inca Trail as well, where we crossed its running flow as an Amazon River tributary via a hanging bridge on the first day of the climb. The terraced cliff sides disappeared and reappeared through the fogs as I soaked in all of the green and the beauty of the mountain, terraces and stone structures.

Many people take the bus to Machu Picchu. I am so glad I hiked into the heart of the Andes via a classic trail. I felt like I was part of the jungle and part of the place in an authentic way, per Immersion Theory.

By fulfilling a young adult dream and exploring a beautiful land and language, I created an immersive global experience full of foods, memories, trials and triumphs. I was hooked on adventure travel and continuing to expand my worldview via learning, seeing, discovering and doing with the three pillars of my life approach.

Mount Rainier: Never Say Never

When I got into mountain climbing I said "Sure, I'll do this, but I never want to do anything with an ice axe, or helmet or crampons. None of that scary dangerous stuff." Then a trip to

Mount Rainier in Washington state came up in America's Pacific Northwest.

Scaling Mount Rainier is known as one of the greatest mountaineering challenges in the contiguous United States. The active volcano is 14,411 feet and full of glaciers, slopes, crevasses, caves and tunnels.

My Mount Rainier trip was completely unlike anything I had ever done before. I was taking on a mountain covered in snow and ice.

It was scary, dangerous and hard to learn the new skills necessary and to climb the mountain. An Army infantry officer who was part of my climbing group on the trip and who had fought in Iraq, said it was the most dangerous place he had ever been. The mountain creates its own weather, kills hikers and has been known to crash aircraft in storms. I knew that the secret to staying alive on this level of climb was to respect the mountain and stay scared.

Getting into this new realm of climbing began as a gear-heavy endeavor. In addition to the usual gear, like the classic 10 hiking essentials, I needed before heading out on a backpack or hiking trip, I learned the five-layer clothing system to stay warm and mobile on extreme peaks. I layered on technical shirts, fleece, softshells, rainproof garments and down. I rounded out my kit with hard-shell mountaineering boots, snow gaiters, poles, a new climbing backpack, a harness, my own ice axe, crampons to attach to my boots, and polarized sunglasses to keep from going snow blind among all the white. I also needed extra down parkas and super-sized crab mitts in my pack for emergencies and a new glove paring with liners and outer shells

I had identified as necessary on Mount Kilimanjaro for the higher altitudes and cold.

This was real mountaineering and I had to develop new ice and snow skills. Mount Rainer required learning self-arrest techniques like stopping myself from falling down the side of a mountain with my ice axe, learning how to climb on steep snow with special duck and rest steps, practicing the ins and outs of connected rope travel and safe crampon use.

On summit day, I went to bed at 6 pm in the Camp Muir bunkhouse after a day of climbing and a horrible just-add-hot-water backpacking meal of beans and rice. I woke up at midnight after struggling to sleep among the many other gear clad campers on the plywood loft in the loud wooden *refugio* with a squeaky door that opened and closed constantly with nervous climbers going in and out on trips to the snow-covered latrine.

We geared in for rope travel and climbed up and up in the dark as snow roared around us. It was July and summer in the northern hemisphere, but the weather on the mountain was full on winter torrent. I had learned that it was hard to eat at high altitude on Mount Kilimanjaro, so this time I had my fueling dialed in with a nutrition drink that I liked the taste of, was easy to digest and included the right mix of protein, carbohydrates and fats. At each break during the dark, storming hiking I would sit down and go into what I call low-power mode: Focusing all my energy on the task at hand, in this case, fueling, while conserving everything else to relax my body when I had a short chance, similarly like I did on the ferry on my way across the Hellespont, saving my energy to swim back. I have used this approach in many more mountain and endurance sports circumstances since, to get through hard events that require everything I have physically and mentally. I eat; I rearrange my clothes and gear; then, I sit and rest in a relaxed position (even when this is often hard to do cliffside), focusing on breathing and the next leg. I don't waste any unnecessary energy.

Our leashed together team continued to career up, gaining elevation. I plunged each step on my tired quad muscles, from the long days trekking, training and hiking before, against a barrage of elements and fear, as the wind howled around my surrounds.

We made it to Disappointment Cleaver at 12,300 feet and the guides called off the climb due to adverse weather: gusty winds, poor visibility and snowing heavily. They would call the weather gnarly. I called it terrifying with wind, enough to knock me down on to the mountain, slammed against my ice axe; enough to wear balaclavas and goggles against the smacking ice pellet snow; enough to hike in our parkas, usually only worn at breaks for warmth; enough to only see white in every direction, hoping there were no lurking crevasses or avalanches nearby.

Going up was hard. Going back down was worse. At some points I decided not to look, trusting in my silent prayers to God, my guides in front of me and the force of the snowy mountain.

While hiking up and down intensely, we had to find the metal *ferratas*, and latch on for connected rope travel, meaning if one climber fell, then we all could as we were connected together against the mountain. It was exhilarating being so close to the edge of such steep drop-offs. Once we got back to Camp Muir, we reunited with those in the group who had turned back early or opted to stay behind before summiting, gathered up the rest of our gear and packs and then used the sliding ski step to get down the remainder of the giant mountain. I had gotten better at this, but it was still nerve racking for me and we were still in a whiteout.

Sometimes you wonder if any of your training is worth it; the early mornings, the missed sleep; the tiredness. As I slid down the mountain on my boots, I had never been more thankful for all of the weight training I had done at the gym. I thought about my friends, classes and the endless squats and knew that my legs were strong enough to get down the mountain. I was thankful for my cross-training and creative movement training, as I needed those muscles.

What I learned on Mount Rainer is never say never. I never thought I wanted to do that kind of climbing, but I had learned the skills necessary and given it my best shot, despite the overwhelming circumstances.

I also learned that it is okay not to reach your goal. We had bad weather on Mount Rainer. It was a dangerous night. Some clear nights, you can walk up the mountain fairly easily, I had heard from other's stories. But I am thankful that we had a true weather experience on the mountain. It was scary and I made the right choice of not being so focused on the goal of the top that I didn't make the right, smart choice to stay within the limits of safety. While I didn't make the summit, I still feel like I had the full Mount Rainer experience. For a month after, when I closed my eyes at night I would see visions of the climb. I would wake frantically with a fright, in my own version of post-traumatic-stress.

This was the kind of weather I didn't want to be immersed in again: Freezing, white knuckle, nerve-wracking white. But I had experienced it; I had explored the mountain and the limits of my skills and abilities at the time. My ultrarun training and the principles of my three pillars allowed me to be in strong physical shape for climbing Mount Rainer. I had more to go on the mental side to become a more skilled and better-prepared mountaineer.

Mount Elbrus & Adaptability

I was left with lingering effects from the stress and intensity of climbing Mount Rainer in the form of nightly dreams of mountain blizzard terrors, but the experience enabled me to go on to scale the highest mountain in Russia, Mount Elbrus, the following summer. Mount Elbrus is the highest mountain in Europe and one of the Seven Summits of the world.

I was successful on Mount Elbrus because I learned the skills I needed on Mount Rainer. I learned how to be comfortable on the mountain. I knew what gear I needed to be physically at ease and what training I needed to be strong. I learned the mountaineering techniques required to be confident in a new environment. I also had acquired the mental and emotional toughness, through the experience of practicing Immersion Theory, to better deal with harsh, intense mountain weather and danger zones. Most importantly, I learned how to adapt to my environment, not unlike cold swimming or distance open water swimming. I was able to adjust myself readily to the different conditions.

Around this time, I also became obsessed with Russian authors. It started years before when I read Dostoyevsky's *Brothers Karamazov*, a book from my dad, and came full circle with a Tolstoy obsession when I picked up *Anna Karenina*, hearkening back to those days in the bookstore as a young adult, where I dreamed about being able to have the patience, time and wherewithal to read a book as big as *War and Peace*.

Now I was embarking on another big adventure, the summiting of a monolith, not dissimilar to reading classic Russian novels, which also require the devotions of time, patience and internal wherewithal.

I had delved into ballet, thanks to a historical fiction book I read while climbing Mount Rainer. I started taking dance class again and learning more about ballet's Russian origins and its demanding physicality of perfection. I was simultaneously training for 100-kilometer and 100-mile ultraruns at the time as well, which allowed me to be in top climbing shape for Mount Rainer and even more so on Mount Elbrus, as I was a summer deep in 100-miler training and running 30 miles, for eight hours at a time, every weekend for months in a row. I was developing my Outlier Tactics and applying them to each endurance sport in turn.

When my dad said he was going to Russia to climb Mount Elbrus, I knew I would do anything to go too, to get to Russia, even if it meant more mountaineering. He wanted to climb this edition of the Seven Summits and was going to Russia to do so. I wanted to go to Russia, and would learn how to climb one of the tallest peaks in the world in order get there, if that is what it took. I wanted to connect with the enigmatic quality that Russians call *Rodina*, which I had read about in my Russian ballet memoirs, classic literature, travelogues and escape feats across Siberia. This Russianness encapsulates the primeval love and attachment that Russians are known for having for their motherland.

The endurance of the mountains had a way of continuing to connect the pieces of my life as I explored art, literature and the apexes of the world. Our visas came in, and after waiting for the final confirmation of those, I knew I was actually going to Russia. My Russian novels and history books were read. I watched Doctor Zhivago and adventure documentary films on the taiga and the Ballets Russes. I drank tea from a samovar. I thrilled my husky with tales of his arctic heritage. My ice axe was back.

I always traveled with waterproof North Face gear bags in a rainbow of colors. On this trip I chose colors that reminded me of the majestic purple mountains I was traveling to, and the wooden greens pines of the Caucasus I would hike in, as I learned to live on and in the mountain, activating my color therapy principles. My medium purple bag served as my carry on and my large green one worked for my checked baggage where I stored my double lined hard-shell mountaineering boots and my sharps: ice axe, crampons and knife. I also packed my helmet, harness, expedition food, my five-layer based clothing system I had learned on Mount Rainer to survive cold mountain life and a multitude of other gear items and appurtenances needed for two weeks on the other side of the world.

Two adventure friends joined us on this two-week trip that included Moscow, Saint Petersburg and Mount Elbrus in the Caucasus Mountain area. I loved the amazing cities and countryside vistas of Russia. I loved the mountain and I loved all the people we met. Most of all, I loved traveling to somewhere that as a child had captivated me.

My Russia campaign was about being comfortable in any situation: a middle seat on an eight-hour flight; navigating the steamy Moscow subway at night; living in a dirty metal barrel hut on a Russian mountain with half-working chairlifts surrounded by scattered Soviet metal debris; dealing with less than ideal facilities on the mountain and off; not coming undone when my eyes were watering, my goggles were foggy, my nose was running, my hands were cold and there was still more climbing to do; being patient; having fun; relaxing and living in the moment—however wonderful or less than it was.

I found that the key to surviving mountaineering was having fun.

One of the things that made climbing Mount Elbrus and the journey fun was the international group that converged together on the mountain. Our climbing team consisted of the four of us from Kansas, another American from Utah, and individuals from Spain, the UK, Japan, Israel, South Africa, Germany, Norway and our two Russian guides.

We were near Sochi, where the Winter Olympics would later be in 2016, when we were climbing Mount Elbrus in 2012. We had planned to climb Elbrus the year before, the year I climbed Mount Rainer, but the trips were cancelled due to terrorists bombing the mountain chairlifts in this conflict area.

The climb was 10 days total, with room for acclimatization training and extra days in case of bad weather, but luckily, we were able to make the summit on our first planned summit day.

Our acclimatizing started with hikes to nearby peaks, then we moved on to the base of Mount Elbrus that we reached via several sections of what looked like abandoned chairlifts, including some of the only one-seaters remaining in the world. These were candy-colored and looked like something left over from the 1960s. We further acclimatizing for several more days by hiking on the glacier to practice, surrounded by gorgeous, strutting and timeless peaks, much denser, pointier and higher than anything I had seen in Colorado.

On the mountain, we lived in the iconic Russian white, blue and red painted metal barrels, but the first day we arrived everything was mistakenly full, so we all had to move into temporary quarters. The men crowded into one massive body-to-body metal structure and us girls bunked with the local cooks, while my dad moved into the camp administrator's filthy, ancient bunkhouse. Our mountain kitchen was a small trailer where devoted young women cooked Russian dishes, like soups and my favorite from the trip, classic Russian salad, for climbers from around the world. It was amazing what fresh delicacies they could conjure up in their tiny space.

Mount Elbrus is said to be home to the world's nastiest outhouse, conferred by Outside Magazine. With all of my worldwide bathroom adventures, it seemed only natural that I go here. It did not disappoint and definitely lived up to its disgusting title.

Other than the dire facilities, and complete lack of while climbing with 10-hour days on end surrounded by the glacial whites and blue of the mountain, the hardest part of the Elbrus climb was being comfortable. I learned how to stay hydrated, but not have to relive myself. It is a skill that has served me well, especially in Patagonia where there were also lots of men around and no facilities. I would envy the males as they could simply go at random, but I learned discipline and it has been helpful on every other ultra and adventure trip. This type of on-location learning was one of those things I did not want to learn until I had to.

Summit day began with a 12:30 am wake-up for an alpine start and a ride on an open-ended Snowcat snowmobile to where we had hiked up to on our training days above a rocky area jutting out above the glacial snow.

We sat packed into each other, crushing against the steepness as we arched up the mountain while the snowplow's tracks rotated under us and the noise drowned out all thoughts and feelings except those of trepidation and nerves. We braced each other, holding ourselves up while not expanding all of our energy for our fast-approaching climb. It was its own crazy, unique excitement, bonded together in the dark hinterlands of the mountain.

The climb itself was not as technical as Mount Rainer, with low visibility and cold, but a manageable endurance climb overall. I had learned that my feet and hands would go numb, despite my layer system that I had developed. That was my hardest challenge mentally. I had to stay calm and not worry or become out of control emotionally that I could not feel my hands and feet. I practiced all my coping mechanisms and focused on keeping my head down and climbing up. Most of the climb was white and snowy. I distinctly remember the steepest parts, where I took leg-zapping steps up the incline of the stalwart summit with snowscapes surrounding me in every direction. All I could see was white. I only focused on the giant nooks in front of me and wiggling my frozen fingers inside my gloves to keep my digits engaged. Hours later once daylight broke, I remember rounding a bend and seeing the false summit. At that moment I felt so happy that I was going to make it to the top! The summit of the highest mountain on the European continent was within my reach.

Once at the top of the official summit, I was greeted by a silver star that reminded me of the soviet stars I saw on top of the buildings in Moscow.

Exploring Russia was a culmination of cultures, endurance, art, skills, friends, family, study and interest. It was extremely moving to climb to the highest point on a continent that encapsulated all these things for me over the course of my life. By finding an endurance sport, and building a wealth of themes I was drawn to around it, I was able to learn new things about the world and see new things in the world by living out Immersion Theory. Once again I used my Outlier Tactics to train for an otherworldly expedition from the plains of Kansas to a former communist republic of states. I used my Explorer's Mindset to take in all things Russia and read copious amounts of Russian history. Tolstoy said that time and patience are the strongest of all warriors. I got to live this out directly in the Caucasus Mountains while mountaineering, using extreme amounts of patience to live in the moment and make the best of it in a raw state. I found the fun, and kept going.

After coming down from Elbrus and celebrating back at the mountain chateaus, it was time to explore Russia's urban side.

Before the climb our group toured Moscow, visiting the Kremlin, Red Square, the GUM shopping arcade and Tolstoy's home. Since I was on a ballet high, we went to the Bolshoi Theater and tried Russian pancakes from a trendy cafe on a cute street near Theater Square.

The city felt so much lighter than I expected, but it still felt Russian with huge apartments everywhere, golden onion domes peaking through the skyline, and Stalin's Seven Sisters skyscrapers bulging around every corner with their enthralling mass and sky-extending spires.

Saint Petersburg was inspired by Venice, Amsterdam, and Paris, and it felt like a mixture of all three with its own special Russian flair—signage in Cyrillic, intricate cathedrals, waterside palaces—under a European sky.

If Moscow was reminiscent of Soviet times, St. Petersburg was reminiscent of the czars.

I took us to various bakeries with our newfound climbing friend from Japan, including those along Nevsky Prospekt. We all made a good climbing team as we had similar interests, like cookies.

We visited the Hermitage, Church of the Savior on Spilled Blood, St. Isaac's Cathedral, Kazan Cathedral, Peter and Paul Fortress and the Mariinsky Theater, among other sights along the city's canals and doubled eagle adornments. We were all more worn out from battling other tourists and taking in art than climbing the mountain.

One of my favorite moments of my time in Russia was taking the hydrofoils across the waters to Peterhof, Peter the Great's complex of palaces and gardens along the Gulf of Finland. It must be because I was once again near the water.

I had adapted to my environment on the mountain and in the former Soviet cities. I learned that adaptability is one of the most important ways to win at life, by overcoming the difficulties of the moment, when at home and abroad.

Canyoneering When There is No Way Out

I now had to ask myself, "Where do you go when you have covered the mountains, the desert and the ocean?"

One of these answers was canyoneering. It was time to go into the earth itself, via Buckskin Gulch, the world's longest slot canyon. It is the deepest slot canyon in the Southwest United States located on the border of Arizona and Utah. That year I had already traveled to the coldest valley in the United States for cross country skiing and snowshoeing in Colorado, and the murder capital of the world in Honduras for tropical ocean swimming, so now I was tackling another one of America's most dangerous hikes in the form of a new endurance sport.

Buckskin Gulch is dangerous because when it rained, it could flash flood, so the trip could get canceled if there were thunderstorms within a 100-mile radius, and there was no way to get out once I started.

My family and I took off for Southern Utah for this 20-mile canyon hike. Canyoneering is the ultimate way to embrace overs, unders and throughs. It combines hiking, swimming and climbing in the form of scrambling and rappelling. It uses endurance and climbing skills to overcome obstacles, drop offs, unknown pools and tiny squeeze-throughs. Each turn through the earth's waves would hold a new adventure and path to navigate through be it rocky land or deep water.

I had been to the purple sunset desert of Arizona and I had been to the orange sand desert of Namibia, but I had never seen the dusky, deserty blues of the northern Arizona American desert before. On my way to hike Buckskin Gulch, I passed through the cactus flowers and sun of Scottsdale, through the scrub brush into the mountains and pines of Flagstaff in the Kaibab National Forest, and back down into the mesas, buttes and soft-focus pastels of the Glen Canyon National Recreation Area for a sunset dinner on Lake Powell. I was captivated by the hazy desert blues. It was a light and landscape all its own.

Lake Powell is a reservoir on the Colorado River. I was venturing here in part to experience the exhilarating story of *The Emerald Mile*, a classic river tale of the attempt to capture the speed record for the fastest boat ride through the Grand Canyon in 1983, first explored by John Wesley Powell in wooden boats in 1869.

The next morning, after being shuttled by my mom, my dad and I set out canyoneering in the deep ochre, undulating slot canyon, full of freezing-water, where I waded in opaque pools up to my waist, then ran fast to warm my legs and feet from the numbing cold water crossings. I climbed over and down rock piles, ran through more rocks or varying sizes, and waded back up through sand and the Paria River, feeling and experiencing the orange walls, narrow tight spots and wide-open amphitheaters of Buckskin Gulch. I had become an ultrarunner and there was no resting, only moving forward through the canyon. My celerity was a sign of training, time and experience.

I had honed how to develop an Explorer's Mindset, use Outlier Tactics and practice Immersion Theory and apply them in all areas of my life to overcome obstacles and find new endurance sports and adventures.

As we exited hours later, we headed out for six more miles of river, more sand hiking and wind back out in the open. If I had to hike in the desert, the best way to enjoy it was to be in a river the whole time.

I had returned to the water.

Back to the Water

A river is inherently dangerous. While I had enjoyed what I learned in the mountains, desert and jungle, my favorite element has always been water, despite its risks.

Another way I found to be in it, via river, was taking a whitewater kayaking course. I had experience with whitewater rafting and flatwater kayaking, but I wanted to expand my skills and abilities.

Whitewater kayaking was a totally different endurance sport than flatwater kayaking. It was like the difference between trail running and road running; mountain biking and road biking; hiking and mountaineering.

I had years of flatwater experience, racing and traveling in canoes, rowing at K-State in college, and kayaking in adventures races; whitewater was all new, with its own set of rules.

The boats were smaller and more maneuverable, tight-fitting, with spots for knees to go up into the boat along the flanks to use your whole lower half for stabilizing and steering as well as your core. Whitewater brought its own gear, as all sport variations do, like a helmet, snug PFD, and chest-high, wetsuit-like skirt that hooked on to the lid of the kayak.

I spent most of this weekend training being wet, not dissimilar to my weeklong Iceland trip several years before, from practicing hip snaps to ear dips to wet exits to swimming in Fontanta Lake and across and down the Tuckasegee River in North Carolina at the Nantahala Outdoor Center.

I was learning so much so fast in this new totally immersive experience; it was a lot to take in mentally and physically. It reminded me of the exhaustion that came from new skills overload on my days training to climb Mount Rainer. In the water, my mind wanted to race when I was underwater, under a boat, waiting for someone to come practice a rescue. The only way to learn how to stay calm in new, life-threating situations like these, was to live them. Immersion Theory was once again at work.

Running and biking used up-and-down hip movement. I liked tapping into more side-to-side hip movement that came with whitewater kayaking. I fell asleep both nights of that weekend training trip twitching, trying to self-correct my balance and feeling like I was still in my kayak.

My favorite part on the river was when our instructor took away our paddles and we had to paddle the kayaks back and forth across the rapids with just our hands a quarter mile. I called it swim boating. I had no idea then how helpful this whitewater experience would be when I would later surf my Arkansas River in Colorado on a stand up paddleboard. Or when I would try out prone boarding during SUP yoga after towing my board behind me while swimming. Finally, I thought, while swim boating, something endurance rather than skill-based!

Because I like endurance sports and think that they can help you win at life, I always create a custom endurance event for my birthday. On my 34th birthday, I decided to complete a distance kayak, on flatwater, on my neighborhood river. I had learned skills, now it was time to apply more endurance. And I wanted to be in the water.

Since I lived near two rivers, The Little Arkansas River and The Big Arkansas River, I started there. These rivers united my framework of endurance sports and tied them and my life together. I spent the spring training in layers of warm, waterproof, ridiculous-looking gear. A new sport once again called for more gear. I woke up early and with the help of my parents, was able to get dropped off 34 miles upstream and kayak down back to my neighborhood. I used the environment around me to create an adventure. Growing up on these rivers, it was remarkable to go farther out into the Kansas countryside, which I had previously only explored via biking and running, and explore it by boat. You always learn a lot on a river; even if it is just a different perspective.

As I paddled through the secluded channel of the watercourse, I took in the sandbars and vivid vegetation that reached out to my watercraft. I spied camps and hideaways and even spotted someone riding a horse bareback on a nearby bank. I spotted my own huge islands in the middle of the river, like the ones I had read about from the Kansas past. I was close to home, but in a new world entirely. On the water I could always discover, explore and find adventure.

To up the ante on local adventure, I have often kayaked at night. In Kansas. Even while pregnant.

On a particular rainy, windy, cold, freezing December 1st night, I took off on a section of the river that is outside of town and that requires navigation. I hiked through mud and portaged over rocks and hills with packrafts and paddles. I got stuck in sandbank shallows: the drama of a prairie river. Getting held up was bad enough in the daylight and sun. During the nighttime cold it was even more stressful to free myself and my boat without expending all of my energy in one frantic burst. But setting off down that river, in the dark, being caught up with the current and completely in nature, one with the wild elements and the dark and the cold and the wet and the sand and the mud. Now that was something truly special. Life is free, if not always easy on the river.

By coming up with ideas outside the norm and going outside to use the elements around me, principles from my pillars, I was once again seeking out adventure via my front door. From around the world, back to my backyard, as long as I was out, I was happy, fulfilled and free.

Endurance & Parenthood

After climbing big mountains, I missed my nearby Colorado 14ers. I wanted to get back to working on my goal of climbing as many of the 58 categorized 14,000-foot mountains as I could.

I had met my husband Parker and we embarked on several Colorado climbs, learning more about ourselves and the mountains on each venture.

In the essence of Tolstoy, I learned that each 14er is a 14er in its own way.

Some 14ers are long hikes; some are steep and dangerous, engirting you like a vice as they narrow and arete; some you meander among aspens, pines and Indian paintbrushes, until you run back down the needled switchbacks, in an attempt to train and push yourself even more; some are big boulder scrambles that you carom through at the top; and some are full of talus and loose rocks, devoid of trees, but not of interest when the marmots and foxes come out. Fourteeners are like the mountains of life.

With our love of the mountains in mind, Parker and I traveled to the Dolomites in Italy for our honeymoon. We combined hiking and climbing into a *via ferrata* travel through World War I bunkers, secret caves and mountain passes in our specialized harnesses, helmets and lanyard-style carabineers. We biked up and down the Alps on mountain ski trails, before hiking, swimming and kayaking across the beachy Cinque Terre and the Mediterranean Sea. We punctured our travels with waterfront hotels, lemon gelatos and cappuccinos, so we didn't suffer any more than we had to, in between our daily endurance challenges—I had learned since backpacking my way through Europe in college. We still had our North Face bags that allowed us to adhere to our unofficial trip theme of Always Be Hiking.

Shortly after, we found out I was pregnant.

I planned my pregnancy announcement by the water. It was November and freezing and I wanted to stand up paddleboard in my wetsuit, mitts and neoprene booties. I needed the water now more than ever.

I was curious to see what my body would be able to handle during pregnancy. I had taken it on several intense journeys already and I wanted to see how that compared to motherhood.

During my second trimester we traveled to Bermuda for a babymoon.

Six hundred miles off the coast of North Carolina in the Atlantic Ocean the island had its own energy thanks to the lure of the infamous Bermuda Triangle. I appreciated the island's history, with its first settlement dating back to 1612.

We hiked long days on beaches we had practically to ourselves and swam in the cold water. One day we coasteered eight miles along the Atlantic coast and connected nine beaches on our own path and then swam out to a 1915 shipwreck. Beach hiking along the soft sand was the best pregnancy activity.

I was able to run through most of my pregnancy. I walked the day I delivered Penelope, and had been working out as normal, with a lowered intensity, up until that day.

I wanted her to know that when I was pregnant with her I continued exploring life and the world around me. Most importantly, I didn't hesitate to jump a few fences, employing an Explorer's Mindset, Outlier Tactics and Immersion Theory to training and to life, whenever necessary.

Our daughter came on the full moon of a 100-year flood.

Water is life. Soothing and violent.

People always ask me how childbirth compares to ultrarunning. It doesn't.

Running is all about forward motion. Progress. Movement.

My childbirth experience was passive. I had to wait for my body to move on its own. There was no amount of willpower or determination that I could employ to make anything happen any faster than time was going to take. I couldn't do anything. I had to stay calm and wait. Moving might ease the pain, but it wouldn't help me get anywhere any faster. There was nowhere to go. During labor I felt like I was floating on a starship to an endless destination in deep space. Pregnancy is like this. You are buoyed up by the creation of life, but also immensely slowed by it.

After traveling around the world running up mountains, crossing deserts, and swimming seas, it was breastfeeding that sent me to the ER.

The patience and organization required for endurance sports and expeditions did help prepare me for parenthood, at least as much as anyone can be prepared for something that changes your life so completely.

In the early days I was exhausted from moving, thinking, planning and never completely resting. Yet my body, so used to endurance, craved more movement. It was hard to stay still, even though that was just what I needed at the time.

Not unlike a well-planned trip, every moment was calculated and accounted for. I had to plan five steps ahead, if not 10, and be organized and prepared for a multitude of possibilities. There were always bags; lots of bags. Everything was queued, triaged and prioritized on an even more extreme level. I lived within a constant revolving revolution of systems.

Having a baby was still about boiled water and linens it turned out; not any different from Medieval or any other time through history. I questioned how the prairie settlers did it daily. I brought up the Kansas pioneers in their dugouts in astonishment. I planned to book a covered wagon history trip through the state's historic Flint Hills and tallgrasses for my daughter after I would read her the *Little House* books as she got older.

I was used to the exhausted sleep of endurance sports, but the sleep of new parenthood was different. After an extreme event, I would be tired and I would sleep, but my mind would cackle awake replaying the day's turns of events, the problem solving, the traumas, learning with bio receptive feedback teaching the body to adapt for the next day. The sleep of parenthood was deep, dark and instant. There was no time or energy to learn or adapt. The blackness of sleep in those early days was survival and immediate, beginning and ending in starts and fits whenever possible.

The balance was elusive.

My first run after pregnancy was hot, hard and pounding. I ran in the afternoon in the middle of the week in July, after getting home from my doctor's office and getting full clearance. It wasn't any more difficult than any other run after a break. I had run through the vagaries of life and ultra training and I knew that I could run through post-partum recovery. I was even more thankful for the freedom and the chance to be me and run outside. When something is taken away from you, you learn to appreciate it even more when you have it back. I knew that it would take time to build my running up, but I could do it because I had done it before. I practiced intuitive running and creative movement. I listened to my body on how, when and why to run, and how to move, enjoying the opportunity to once again be immersed in the outdoors, while enjoying the chance to look for new kinds of adventures.

CONCLUSION

Training For Life

Some things in life find you.

I learned to climb mountains, run volcanoes, trek deserts, hike canyons, bushwhack jungles and swim seas that I dreamed of as a child by cultivating my life training approach of developing an Explorer's Mindset, using Outlier Tactics and practicing Immersion Theory. This approach allowed me to connect with nature, explore and seek adventure, which helped me win personally and professionally, as I became stronger overall.

I needed to find the right sport for the next phase in life. Similarly to after college, I once again returned to multisport. This time, instead of triathlons and adventure races, I combined all of my new sports, skills and distance training into new adventures that I could have and create right at home. It was time for multisport. With my husband Parker and baby Penelope in tow.

It was time for Multisport For Life.